D0976755

Hunting Season

Also by James Harkin

Niche:
The Missing Middle and Why Business Needs to
Specialize to Survive

Cyburbia:
The Dangerous Idea That's Changing How We Live
and Who We Are

Hunting Season

James Foley, ISIS, and the
Kidnapping Campaign
That Started a War

James Harkin

BOOKS

NEW YORK   BOSTON

Hachette Books
Hachette Book Group
1290 Avenue of the Americas
New York, NY 10104

www.HachetteBookGroup.com

Printed in the United States of America

RRD-C

First Hachette Books edition: November 2015
10 9 8 7 6 5 4 3 2 1

Hachette Books is a division of Hachette Book Group, Inc.

The publisher is not responsible for websites (or their content) that are not owned by the publisher.

ISBN: 978-0-316-30517-4
LCCN: 2015947733

To the memory of James Harkin senior

Contents

Mount Sinja

Mosul •

• Raqqa

AQQA

I R A Q

N

Key:
Provinces: *RAQQA*

Living Hell

Kneeling in the desert sands, his orange jumpsuit flapping insistently in the breeze, a shaven-headed forty-year-old struggles to focus on the cameras in front of him and the statement he's meant to recite. It's a press conference of a kind, but the man delivering it has his hands tied behind his back and the words are clearly being forced into his mouth. They announce his imminent execution. He calls on his family and fellow citizens "to rise up against my real killer, the U.S. government," which had apparently sealed his fate with its recent bombing campaign in Iraq. "I wish I could have more time," he says. "I wish I could have the hope of freedom, and seeing my family again. But that ship has sailed. I guess, all in all, I wish I wasn't American."

For a brief moment—after the video exploded onto the internet—no one was quite sure who he was. Why would they be? Jim Foley was a handsome and intrepid journalist, but hardly well known—he worked freelance, for little money and in places others feared to tread. If he was squinting in the sunlight it was not only because he was straining to follow the script; it was because he'd barely seen the sun in the previous two years.

In November 2012 Foley went missing along with another photojournalist, a Briton called John Cantlie, in Northern Syria. The two were firm friends, and together would spend nearly two years being herded around ten different prisons in three different provinces of Northern Syria, most of them underground and the majority abominably cruel. Along with twenty-two other foreign hostages they'd ended up in Raqqa, the de facto capital of the Islamic State of Iraq and Sham (ISIS), and in the hands of the most notorious group of prison guards.

One of those guards took a starring role in the video; a black-clad, brown-skinned narrator to Foley's left, gesturing at the camera with his knife. Stocky, with his face obscured by a balaclava, the guard was clearly British, and speaking in a London accent. Armed for effect with an expensive Glock pistol, the killer harangued his audience on the evils of the American government. "You're no longer fighting an insurgency," he said. "We are an Islamic army and a state that has been accepted by a large number of Muslims worldwide." As the speeches drew to a close, Foley gritted his teeth and clenched his jaw before the killer began slicing through his throat. The camera faded to black. The next sequence showed Foley's bloodied head posed neatly on his back.

The entire video lasted for two hundred and eighty seconds, but Jim Foley's part took up only eighty-five of them. It appeared on YouTube on August 19, 2014, but is thought to have been filmed the day before.[1] Watch closely: it was stitched

---

1. According to an article written under duress by John Cantlie for *Dābiq*, the Islamic State magazine, in October 2014.

together from different takes; the filming must have taken several hours. At one point the picture became a split-screen. A flashy preamble reprised a speech that President Obama had made two weeks earlier, announcing American air strikes in Iraq.

Obama's intent was to halt the advance of a brand-new terror army, whose ranks of hardened jihadis had been swollen by volunteers from all around the world, and whose sandal-wearing blitzkrieg through Northern Iraq two months earlier had already seen them conquer the country's second city, Mosul. But the result was to provoke the ire of the Islamic State, and to put the lives of its Western hostages in grave danger.

At the end of the video Steven Sotloff, another freelance journalist, appeared, held by the scruff of another orange jumpsuit. Two weeks later, in an almost identical video, he was decapitated by the same British jihadi.

On August 19 Diane and John Foley were at home in Rochester, New Hampshire. It was a normal day, in so far as anything in the Foley household could be called normal since their oldest son had vanished in Northern Syria. For almost two years, they turned over every possible scenario and sat down with just about everyone, from the American State Department to the Syrian Ambassador to the United Nations, in an effort to get him back. They had also been turned over themselves; like some of the other families of the hostages, having their son taken gave them a crash course in the kidnapping industry, its inventive storytelling, its shameless money-grubbing and its downright duplicity. For a long time they had no idea whether Jim was even alive or dead. It threw their lives entirely upside down, shattering their comfortable, leafy existence like a bomb.

At last, however, there were grounds for cautious optimism. Between March and June of 2014 fifteen European hostages being held alongside Foley were freed in a series of deals brokered among European governments, insurers and families. For the Foleys, one of the worst things was not knowing what ISIS wanted; recently, however, its motives seemed to have become more transparent: they wanted money. In early August, Diane Foley went on her own to Europe to meet some of the freed hostages. In Copenhagen she'd spent time with Daniel Rye Ottosen, the Danish photographer who'd been released in June and who'd become a friend to Jim in captivity. After that she'd traveled to Paris to drum up support in the American Embassy there. A prominent Syrian opposition activist had offered to try to open up a line of communication between the U.S. government and the Islamic State, and Diane was quietly hopeful. "Finally, I thought, maybe someone can help," she told me. In Paris, she also spent the weekend with another two hostages who'd been with Jim in the prison, Pierre Torres and Didier François, and discussed fresh ideas for how to get Jim out.

While Diane was away, an email arrived from the kidnappers. John read it to her over the phone: a badly spelled, crazily capitalized tirade directed at the U.S. government and its citizens as much as them. "HOW LONG WILL THE SHEEP FOLLOW THE BLIND SHEPPARD?" Their Western hostages, it claimed, had "DARED TO ENTER THE LION'S DEN AND

WHERE EATEN!" Then came the threat: "You and your citizens will pay the price of your bombings! The first of which being the blood of the American citizen, James Foley! He will be executed as a DIRECT result of your transgressions toward us!" The tone of this email was strikingly different from the sometimes-friendly emails they'd received nine months earlier, and which had dried up almost as soon as they began. But so desperate were the Foleys and their advisers to open a channel of communication with the kidnappers that they were inclined to see this new email as another reason for cautious hope.

It didn't last long. Diane and John Foley remembered nothing unusual about the early part of August 19, except for one detail. At some point in the morning a car rolled up to the house and FBI agents presented themselves at their door; polite and business-like, they requested a family DNA sample, but didn't say why. Three hours later, Diane remembered the phone ringing and a journalist acquaintance of Jim's being on the end of it, utterly hysterical after seeing the video online. It was on TV within the hour. After that, their whole world caved in, and the global media turned up on their doorstep. The Pope telephoned to pay his respects. So did President Obama, who expressed his condolences and revealed—effectively declassifying it—that a rescue mission had taken place six weeks previously, but came back empty-handed. The presidential phone call was especially poignant because Jim, a long-time Democrat, had worked hard to get Barack Obama elected in 2008 and had confidence in his judgment. "Jimmy believed until the very end that his government would come to save him," John Foley told me, and when the President phoned, the elder

Foley told him exactly that. "I got no response, but I wanted him to know. That's when he told me he felt deeply sorry."

If the Foley's pleas for help had largely fallen on deaf ears when Jim was alive, all that changed after his death. His public execution, and those that followed, had immediate consequences. The killings ignited a furious debate about the merits of Obama's decision to intervene in Iraq, and whether the administration could have done more to protect kidnapped Americans in Syria. The Obama administration was clearly reluctant to engage militarily in the region, but the effect of Foley's killing on public opinion forced its hand. While only one in five Americans had backed air strikes against the Syrian regime in 2013, two thirds now backed American air strikes against ISIS in its home base of Northern Syria. This "new public hawkishness," said *The Economist*, "is linked to the reporters' beheading, pollsters report. Americans paid more attention to those murders than to any other news event in the past five years, according to one survey." No one had paid much attention to Jim Foley's plight while he was alive. But it's no exaggeration to say that his murder helped push America into exactly what many of its people had been trying to avoid—an open-ended regional war against a ruthless, implacable new enemy.

The revolt against the Syrian regime wasn't supposed to turn out like this. When it erupted in March 2011 it started peaceably enough, inspired by protests in other Arab countries and organized by a fresh generation of activists around mosques, local communities and new media. The aim was to topple Syria's tired, oppressive old security state and its president, Bashar al-Assad, who had been gifted the top job after the death of his father. After the Syrian army and its paramilitary allies cracked down hard, informal bands of defectors sprung up to protect their communities and the revolt became a military street fight. The Syrian army triumphed, but it was a hollow victory. As the defectors retreated, a new wave of religiously inspired militants, buttressed by an international brigade of jihadis from every corner of the world, took their place. The country's once-hopeful rebellion atrophied into carnage and religious hatred.

One symptom of Syria's spiral out of control was the growing number of kidnappings of foreign journalist and aid workers. Jim Foley and John Cantlie were two of the first to go, in November 2012. For much of the following two years, I'd been investigating their whereabouts: it seemed to me a good and important story, all the more so because hardly any other journalists were looking into it with any seriousness. It was also a forest of false trails and spurious tips, with a cast of characters stranger than anything I'd come across in fiction. There were good reasons why a reporter like me should be interested in the fate of missing journalists. I'd traveled to exactly the same places they had and run into many of the same people; finding out how they disappeared from the face of the earth took on the urgency of self-preservation. Encouraged by several generous commissions from *Vanity Fair*, and in between my regular reporting trips to Syria and Iraq, my interest in the kidnappings grew alongside my determination to understand the people who seemed to be behind them. By the time of Foley's death I was one of a small number of people who knew for sure who was holding him and many other foreign hostages, this brand-new organization calling itself the Islamic State.

Two days after the Foley video was posted on YouTube, in my local coffee bar in London, I met two former ISIS hostages. Pierre Torres and Daniel Rye Ottosen, both European photographers, were among the last friendly faces to see Foley alive. Both were shell-shocked; the same thing might easily have happened to them. While Torres and Ottosen had agreed to meet me, neither wanted to say much for publication. They had their reasons. Their British jihadi guards had threatened that if they spoke to journalists those left behind in captivity would suffer terrible consequences. "If we start to talk, it will give them a good excuse," Ottosen told me. Some of the hostages had even made a pact with one another to shut up until everyone got out. Others just didn't want to replay terrible memories for the general public.

I respected this reasoning, but I begged to differ. After all, bringing back the truth was why some of these men and women had gone to Syria in the first place. As the taking of hostages became endemic in the Syrian conflict, blacking out information and swearing people to secrecy seemed like a terrible way to solve the problem, as well as a dereliction of journalistic duty. I kept coming back to Jim Foley, whose kidnapping and execution—he was one of the first to go missing, and the first to be executed—seemed to bookend the whole unfathomably tragic series of events.

As I continued down the rabbit hole of hunting out information on kidnapping, I became convinced that something wasn't right about the official story of who was behind it; it didn't help that everyone seemed to be squirrelling away information or actively concealing it. At the time, the Foley abduction was so puzzling that it looked like an outlier, but as whisperings of similar kidnappings trickled in it became clear that something much bigger than we realized was afoot. This wasn't an outlier but an omen—of the way that the Syrian conflict was going, of our tragic failure to understand and influence foreign conflicts, of our reckless lack of intelligence about what was really happening on the ground.

There were more specific questions too, which daily news reporting hadn't even begun to answer. Such as how could Jim Foley and John Cantlie have found themselves in an ISIS prison when the group hadn't even been in existence at the time they had gone missing? And how could it be that the masked Londoner who decapitated Foley on video had also been involved in his kidnapping nearly two years earlier?

CHAPTER ONE

Open Season

In the late afternoon of July 19, 2012 the British freelance photojournalist John Cantlie paced the lobby of his hotel in Antakya, Turkey, twenty kilometers from the border, and made urgent noises into his mobile phone. Together with a Dutch photographer friend Jeroen Oerlemans, he was planning to sneak into rebel-held Northern Syria via the country's long, porous boundary with Turkey. The journey would involve bouncing along in a pick-up truck to a safe house near the border, waiting until word came that the coast was clear, then racing up and down a series of rocky hills as fast as their equipment would allow. Everything had to be done in the dark, and in perfect silence, to avoid a beating at the hands of the Turkish border police.

This was to be Cantlie's second trip inside. On his first, earlier that year, he'd gone with his friend Jim Foley who knew the area well. This time Foley was already in Northern Syria, and getting great stuff. Events on the ground were changing fast. Since Foley and Cantlie's previous visit, Syria's civilian uprising had entirely given way to an armed rebellion led by a loose franchise called the Free Syrian Army. As Syria's regular army leaked men and morale, the rebels had grown in confidence, and their guerilla campaign was now moving out of the countryside and into the two major cities, Damascus and Aleppo, the twin citadels that the regime could not afford to lose.

The previous day, they'd received a breathtaking morale boost: three of President Bashar al-Assad's closest military advisers had been killed in a bomb attack inside the National Security headquarters in Damascus. Now attention had moved north to Aleppo, where a shifting tapestry of Islamist militias was preparing for an ambitious assault on Syria's second city. If Cantlie and Oerlemans didn't get in soon, they were in danger of being left behind.

At the last minute, however, they encountered a hitch. Mustafa, the Syrian guide Jim Foley and John Cantlie had used the last time, couldn't make it to the border, but had sent his young cousin, a shy ex-solider in the Syrian army called Durgham, to meet them instead. It was while Cantlie phoned these logistical changes around that I saw him in the foyer of the hotel. We'd chosen the same musty, mid-priced Antakya dive, the Mozaik, and the same route into Syria—only I was on my way out. That morning, at a magnificent stone mansion overlooking a tomato garden on the Syrian side of the border, I'd interviewed the rebel commander of the whole region, a mustachioed, former colonel in the Syrian army.

Just a stone's throw from where we were sitting, the rebels were battling to take control of the strategically important border crossing of Bab al-Hawa. The previous evening, the son of my Syrian host, a thin, pious-looking man in his early twenties, had fetched me dinner, a brand-new assault rifle slung over his shoulder, and then driven off with his friends to have another crack at the border post. When I asked the commander whether he'd seen any foreign jihadis in the area, however, he told me he hadn't encountered a single one. He couldn't have been looking very hard. Later that day the rebels did indeed take the crossing at Bab al-Hawa, but only in an operation led by an obscure new battalion heavy with foreign jihadis who'd come fight the Syrian regime, called Majlis Shura al-Mujahideen, or the Mujahideen Shura Council; sometimes they simply called themselves Dawla Islamiya—Islamic State. Flush with victory, and in footage which still exists on You-Tube, their emir struts along the checkpoint tarmac declaring "the establishment of an Islamic State" flanked by a few non-Syrian Arabs; one carries the white-circle-on-black flag which would later become famous as the logo of ISIS.

At almost exactly the same time, a few kilometers away, it was John Cantlie and Jeroen Oerlemans's bad luck to stumble into their base camp. As the men picked along the boulders on their way into Northern Syria they could hear bullets and the whirring of regime helicopters as the rebels advanced on the border crossing at Bab al-Hawa. A row of rebel tents looked like the perfect place to break their journey, and Durgham suggested they ask for a cup of tea. It was a mistake; within thirty seconds bearded, dark-skinned men were all around them, toting guns and haranguing them for being spies. When Durgham tried to speak on their behalf in Arabic, Cantlie was astonished to hear a voice booming out of the darkness in perfect London-accented English: "I'm going to kill this guy if he doesn't shut up."

The Brits, of whom there were at least half a dozen, soon proved to be the biggest threat to Cantlie and Oerlemans. They were much more brutal than the others and kept insisting that the two journalists deserved imminent execution. One, whom the journalists named the Preacher, suggested that they "Prepare for the afterlife. Are you ready to meet Allah?"

From under his blindfold Oerlemans could make out another tall British man wearing trainers and a shiny tracksuit. He reminded Oerlemans of the young Arabs he'd seen smoking shisha on the streets of west London's Edgware Road. "Someone with the manners of a city boy, and who thinks he knows it all." He was also sadistic, forcing the journalists to sit with their hands cuffed behind their backs for long periods, and generally manhandling and humiliating them for his own satisfaction. "He was clearly frustrated; he immediately hated us. He was from Britain, and therefore he hated Britons. I don't know why but he must have felt alienated—envious. He was talking about our rotten society in general; it was all about us being *kafirs*, or unbelievers, who don't know what we're talking about. And that we're going to be for it now."

By day two, thoroughly spooked by the fervor of their captors, the journalists decided to make a run for it. In a vivid dispatch he wrote afterward for the *Sunday Times*, John Cantlie recounted what happened next: "I ended up running for my life, barefoot and handcuffed, while British jihadists—young men with south London accents—shot to kill. They were aiming their Kalashnikovs at a British journalist, Londoner against

Londoner in a rocky landscape that looked like the Scottish Highlands. Bullets kicking up dirt as I ran. A bullet through my arm, another grazing my ear. And not a Syrian in sight." Shot and wounded, Oerlemans and Cantlie were dragged back to the camp to be tormented even more. At one point Cantlie heard the sharpening of knives. When news came that the pair might be ransomed rather than killed, they took it as a relief.

At the time, John Cantlie's first encounter with British jihadis in Syria was thought by some Syria journalists to be an unfortunate hiccup in the course of a conflict about other things. The one thing everyone could agree upon was that it wasn't really a kidnapping at all. "They were as surprised as we were," Jeroen Oerlemans told me. "We walked into their camp, and maybe they saw an opportunity." In retrospect there was something amateurish about the whole thing—Cantlie would later dub it "an adventure course for disenchanted twenty-year-olds"—but it was also evolving into something else. The reason they'd made a run for it, according to Oerlemans, was that "we didn't want to end up in orange jumpsuits": the fate of some Western hostages of al-Qaeda during the early years of the Iraq war, shortly before their grisly execution. The journalists' ordeal only ended when friendly local rebels barged into the camp and demanded their release.

"They were so fucking religious," remembers Oerlemans. "All the talk was about what heaven would look like. You'd be taken to Paradise, where Allah would preside on a huge throne—your family would already be there, and there'd be lots of girls." Before that, however, there was work to be done. The foreign jihadis, as those who rescued the journalists explained, badly wanted to take the border crossing so they could use it as a bridgehead to bring more of their comrades into Syria. "First we have to fight the regime in Syria," is how Oerlemans remembers their plan of attack, "then there will be something much bigger; we will have to fight the Western crusaders. It will be the war to end all wars, the final reckoning and the last battleground." It was the British guys who were saying this. When he read the first issue of *Dābiq*, the Islamic State's magazine, two years later, it felt to Oerlemans that it had been written by the same people.

The abduction of friendly foreign journalists like John Cantlie was a surprise to everyone. A year earlier, Syria had been a country reborn. Riding the wave of hope that was the Arab Spring, thousands took to the streets to demand greater freedoms and an end of pervasive corruption. Fear fell away: as the protests gathered momentum, it looked like Syria might finally break the iron rod with which the Assad family and its Ba'athist regime had ruled the country for more than forty years. The rush of adrenaline—that sense of history in the making—was infectious, and made ordinary people take risks they wouldn't otherwise have considered.

Journalists, too. While John Cantlie was being kicked and threatened with death by British jihadis, Jim Foley, who worked mainly for *GlobalPost* and the French news agency AFP, was being spirited into regime-held Aleppo by some of its university students. It was dangerous work. Foley and his photographer friend Nicole Tung had to pass through Syrian army checkpoints, keeping their mouths firmly shut to not draw attention in the back of the car. Their hosts were taking enormous risks to protect them, and in return they trusted them with their lives. "These people knew what they were doing," Tung remembers. "They knew what to do to get us through."

My own first encounter with Syria's youthful revolutionaries had taken place earlier that year. I'd gone back to Syria in February 2012 to catch up with a dissident I'd met on a previous visit to the country. Let's call him Yasser. When I first met him Yasser was a cynical chain-smoker and a loosely employed politico who was hostile to the Syrian regime, but who laughed off the idea that the civil unrest then brewing in Iran could ever make its way to his country. But the Arab Spring had transformed him, and now he organized an interview for me with two fledgling members of the rebel Free Syrian Army in the heart of Damascus's Old City. We needed to be careful. Four months earlier my friend Sean McAllister, who was working as a journalist in Damascus without permission, had been dragged off the street by Syrian state security; he'd been deported after a few days in prison, but some of the activists he'd been working with were still in prison.

Unfailingly polite, yet grim-faced—they risked summary execution if apprehended by the authorities—the men I met from the Free Syrian Army explained their defection as the direct result of observing the brutal military response to civilian demonstrations at the beginning of the Syrian uprising the previous March. These soldiers had no appetite for killing civilians, and they'd broken away from the army, like Mustafa's cousin Durgham. They made contact with other groups of defectors and together sought to protect their communities from the security forces and *shabiha*, their gun-toting paramilitary allies. As their numbers grew, their operations grew bolder and the regular army retreated. Now, under the nose of the authorities and in the total darkness of a power outage, they were here to ask the outside world for guns—it was, interrupted Yasser on their behalf, all they needed to finish the job.

Elsewhere in Damascus demos were being organized almost every day, always on the hoof and often by young activists who'd already been arrested and brutalized for their efforts. At one, I tagged along with legions of young people between the ages of ten and twenty-five, following a funeral procession for a boy who'd apparently been shot by the security forces. Walking through the narrow streets of Kafr Sousa with his body held aloft, surrounded on all sides by walls of *shabiha* and the acrid smell of tear gas, the energy and discipline of the protesters was breathtaking; this was the most impressive display of people power I'd ever seen.

It didn't last long. As the crowd pushed forward, the *shabiha* charged and everyone dashed for cover into the surrounding side streets. I followed a young Syrian man, both of us pelting down a dusty alleyway for about a hundred yards before we looked behind and saw no one was coming. As our sprint gave way to a stroll I asked him whether he resented the country's religious minorities, many of whom didn't seem to be taking any interest in the uprising or were quietly taking the government's side. "Our revolution isn't a sprint, it's more like a marathon," he'd answered, imitating the labored jogging of a

long-distance runner. "Some people are there from the beginning, and many others join only halfway through. But by the
finish line we're all going to be moving at the same pace, and
running along together."

It didn't happen. One reason why Syria's revolt spiraled out
of control is that some of its revolutionaries spent too much
time soliciting foreign support and not enough convincing
their fellow citizens to turn their back on the devil they knew.
Another was that, on its fringes, there was a festering sense of
resentment among the country's impoverished Sunni Muslim
majority.

A few days after the demo I accompanied Yasser and a
taxi driver on a whistle-stop tour of another area of Damascus, where thousands had turned out for a demo a few days
earlier only to be fired upon by plain-clothes security men.
We'd sped through the nest of alleys from which the protesters had emerged and a rough-looking security man appeared
from nowhere wielding a club, like a low-resolution thug from
some ancient computer game. There'd been almost no one on
the streets, but the graffiti was still visible. In among the usual
injunctions to freedom was the assertion that "Aroor is praying for us." Adnan al-Aroor, an exiled Syrian preacher living
in Saudi Arabia, had been using his cable-TV pulpit to preach
a message of Sunni extremism, and threatening that Muslims
from the Alawi sect, who formed the bedrock of support for
the regime of President Assad, would be "turned into mince-
meat and fed to the dogs" if they fought back. Syria's revolt
wasn't all peace and love, and while it was hard for visiting
journalists to see—most were banned by the Syrian regime,
and the few who were allowed to work did so under constant

supervision—the country was becoming a magnet and a new cause célèbre for Islamic extremism.

Even before anyone was kidnapped, Syria was the most dangerous place in the world for journalists. Scores had been killed. One of the most high profile was Marie Colvin, an American reporter who was killed in a blizzard of shells on February 22, 2012, after the Syrian army launched a full-scale assault on rebel areas of the city of Homs.

I was in Syria when it happened, and had co-written one of her last articles for the *Sunday Times*. Six days after Colvin's death I traveled to Homs to find out what was going on, and was briefly arrested by the Syrian army. After her death, the foreign media, already hampered by dwindling budgets, drew back from covering the conflict. It didn't stop a lightly resourced, risibly paid, almost wholly uninsured brigade of freelancers, often armed with little more than a notebook and a mobile phone, from charging across the Turkish border anyway. A few were crazy narcissists or war-zone tourists, but most were real reporters moved to find out more about a conflict that their professional curiosity or overwhelming ambition wouldn't allow them to ignore.

Two of them were Jim Foley and John Cantlie. I was another. In the lonely band of Syria journalists, like BASE jumpers or high-wire walkers, everyone quickly became familiar with everyone else. The necessity to stick together often ran far ahead of the instinct for competition. On a foray into Northern Syria the week before John Cantlie's first abduction in July 2012, I'd rolled up at a disused football pitch only to find two glazed-looking Eastern European journalists sunning themselves outside an impromptu media office. One was heavily bearded, and it looked like both had been living there for months. The building they were sitting outside had been shot up by a helicopter from a nearby regime airbase; it looked like a scene from *Apocalypse Now*. All the same, they'd been sleeping on its roof. A day or two after I got there two more freelancers would arrive to share the roof—Jim Foley and Nicole Tung. One of the Eastern Europeans, a Hungarian reporter called Balint Szlanko, knew Jim from Afghanistan and Libya; they'd met at airports and military camps, "in the small spaces between war, the bubbles of peace amid all the mayhem." Now they were with two others on a random roof, talking about war and ice cream.

A month earlier, stranded in the suburbs of Homs, Jim Foley had run into another American, Austin Tice. On May 23, this intrepid thirty-year-old freelancer had crawled under a fence into Northern Syria. Tice hadn't published a single article, but it didn't matter. He'd spent time in Egypt, and been hugely inspired by the revolution against President Hosni Mubarak, which saw hundreds of thousands of people congregate in and around Cairo's Tahrir Square. Now Syria was the story that everyone wanted—all the more so because, with the Syrian government keeping a tight rein on visas, hardly anyone was there. Tice was a former Marine captain with tours of Afghanistan and Iraq under his belt, but now his ambition was to go back to the region with a fresh pair of eyes and force open a new career as a photojournalist. Most of his favorite books were by war reporters—in particular *For Whom the Bell Tolls*. He'd even brought a few of them to read along the way.

The next three months would surpass Tice's wildest fantasies of Ernest Hemingway. His companion and guide for most of it, Mahmoud, was a bespectacled Syrian in his early fifties—wiry and stubborn, a bit like an older, shorter, Syrian version of Austin himself. The two met via mutual friends and bonded quickly, as people in war zones are prone to do. Tice would poke fun at Arab procrastination and Mahmoud would call him "White Boy."

Until a few months earlier, Mahmoud had been in the U.S., leasing out industrial equipment in Atlanta; now he was a soldier in the newly minted Free Syrian Army and well on his way to becoming a brigade commander. Things were changing fast, and it was possible to believe that before long the rebels would be in Damascus and Syria's creaking Ba'athist regime would go the same way as Muammar Gaddafi's had in Libya. Two days in, Austin and Mahmoud cut a swathe through the dangerous terrain of Northern Syria and made it to a rebel base in Hama: "Writing like a maniac" wrote Tice on Twitter, "taking photos, working like crazy."

Tice turned out to be a gifted journalist. Laid out in scattershot bursts on Flickr and on Twitter, mixing field maneuvers with the Free Syrian Army with references to country pop, Tice's social media trail made for a thrilling, hard-charging alternative to the flak-jacketed puppetry of much war-zone reporting—an exhilarating gonzo ride through the Syrian rebellion as it gathered confidence and momentum. He bantered about football with rebels from Homs, drew on his military background to produce a forensic analysis of the weapons and strategy of both sides, and ribbed the *New York Times* along with the rest of the international media for its inability to put a journalist on the ground ("Srsly guys if any of y'all wanna come down here, I would love some company").

Then there was the time he made it through a Syrian army checkpoint wearing an ill-fitting burqa that was supposed to reach the ground but which, on his lanky six foot three frame, did not come close to covering his hands and feet. The soldiers he strolled past weren't impressed either, and began shooting at him as he zigzagged down the street. His headstrong, impudent side wasn't to everyone's taste—on at least one occasion his rebel hosts had to put him under house arrest for his own safety. "Tonight made a good-faith effort to explain gay rights to a fun and well-meaning group of Syrian guys," he wrote at one point. "Yeah, not the time, not the place." When a young rebel, struggling for a cultural referent, kept following him around singing "Jingle Bells," Tice had to tell him to shut the fuck up.

Mahmoud left the central Syrian province of Homs to go back to the fighting in Northern Syria, after which Tice was passed from tiny battalion to tiny battalion, making friends quickly and trusting those he met with his life. It was at this time that he'd met Jim Foley. For ten days, according to two Syrians who were with them, the two stayed up late into the night talking about anything and everything. Tice spent much of it shooting his mouth off about the amateurism of the Free Syrian Army, and Foley had to calm him down.

In July, Tice made it to Yabroud, a city north of Damascus, and his cocky adventurism reached new heights. "Not to be arrogant," he wrote to Mahmoud on Facebook, "but lots of women love me here." Yabroud was where he learned how to drink Syria-style, where he landed his first article in the *Washington Post* and where, according to Mahmoud, he fell in love.

Tice dated a Syrian woman for several weeks, but she already had a fiancé and Mahmoud wrote to warn him that "they are going to kick your ass." It was around this time, too, that Tice penned a kind of mission statement, setting out what he was trying to achieve on his Facebook page:

> We kill ourselves every day with McDonald's and alcohol and a thousand other drugs, but we've lost the sense that there actually are things out there worth dying for. We've given away our freedoms piecemeal to robber barons, but we're too complacent to do much but criticize those few who try to point out the obvious. Americans have lost their sense of vision, mistaking asinine partisan squabbles for principles. When we do venture into space—the part of space we've gotten comfortable with, mind you—now we pay the Russians to give us a ride. That's humiliating. I can't believe we let that happen.
>
> So that's why I came here to Syria, and it's why I like being here now, right now, right in the middle of a brutal and still uncertain civil war. Every person in this country fighting for their freedom wakes up every day and goes to sleep every night with the knowledge that death could visit them at any moment. They accept that reality as the price of freedom [...] They're alive in a way that almost no Americans today even know how to be. They live with greater passion and dream with greater ambition because they are not afraid of death.

The threats were coming in more regularly now, and from peculiar new directions. Tice made it through to Damascus in late July, where for two weeks he fell in with another hospitable group of rebels in the suburb of Darraya. All the same, he couldn't help worrying about the growing attacks on journalists; on hearing what had happened John Cantlie and Jeroen Oerlemans he tweeted that, "for obvious reasons, I find this recent trend of attacks against media targets to be troubling, to say the least." At one point he bugged his hosts to take him to an adjoining but more contested area called Jdeidat Artouz, which was thick with spies and paranoia. Islamists may have tried to arrest him there, but his rebel friends apparently kept him safe; even so the experience clearly freaked him out. "Pervasive fear of spies," he wrote in one of the tweets he left behind. "Unlike any other place I've visited. Creepy." Tice made it back to Darraya on August 11, in time for his thirty-first birthday, where his final tweet was characteristically upbeat: "Spent the day at an FSA pool party with music by @taylorswift13. They even brought me whiskey. Hands down, best birthday ever." Two days later, he disappeared.

Six weeks after Tice went missing, a forty-seven-second video popped up on the internet, apparently showing him on a mountainside, blindfolded and being taunted by Islamic extremists. The production values, the freshly laundered, Afghan-style clothes of the supposed Islamists, even the way they chanted "Allahu Akbar" (God is Great), all seemed out of kilter, as if its producers were engaged in a deliberate parody. Just about every independent analyst smelled a rat; since the Syrian regime's central propaganda claim was that it was battling al-Qaeda, its agents had every reason to show an American in jihadi captivity. I buzzed one of the young rebels on the Turkish–Syrian border who'd spent time with Austin while he was there; by the time the video appeared he was back in the suburbs of Damascus and, in his spare time, trying to figure out what had happened. "Faked," was the verdict on the video. "Now we know he is with the regime."

This is how it goes. Blindfolded, with your hands tied behind your back, you're manhandled into the backseat of a car. With your head forced down into the brace position, burly *shabiha* pressing into your flesh on either side, you can't see a thing. But hearing is enough. What you can hear is the vehicle being driven scarily fast to avoid the attentions of rebels, and thumping militaristic pop as your captors sing along to "God, Syria and Bashar" on the radio. In the sinister revelry you attract a few slaps on the back of the head. After what seems like some hours you're pushed out of the car at a military airport amid the whirring of helicopter blades. A few hours later you're in Damascus and being driven at full throttle to a security compound in the center of the city, where you're deposited in your own tiny concrete cell deep underground. By now it's dawned on you that you're booty. For the first few days your interrogators toy with you, affecting to think you're a spy. Soon, however, you realize it's more an exercise in form-filling and you learn to bide your time. It's easier said than done; since you're blindfolded or in your cell at all times you have no idea whether it's day or night.

That's if you've been taken by the Syrian regime at all. The truth is that there are *shabiha* on both sides of Syria's conflict. The term is thirty years old, and originally referred to gangs of smugglers along Syria's borders whose excellent regime connections gave them license to do as they pleased. Since the outbreak of the uprising many simply transferred their loyalties to the Free Syrian Army and began running arms instead. In the many relationships that grease palms along Syria's traditional smuggling routes, it wasn't always clear what the allegiances of armed men really were, or if they had any loyalties at all. For some of these gangs, kidnapping for ransom was already a way of life; war-ravaged Syria made it a flourishing business.

In the early stages of the conflict Syria's rebel armies had been happy to protect visiting journalists with their lives; if the world could see the iniquities of the regime, they reckoned, the Western powers could be chivvied into large-scale military intervention on their behalf. When that didn't happen, some found a more creative use for the journalists slipping through Syria's borders—as commodities to be traded for cash. If they could pin it on the Syrian regime, even better.

In March 2013 the BBC's *World Affairs* correspondent Paul Wood was crossing the border from Lebanon with a group of rebel-friendly smugglers when he and three of his colleagues were abducted by masked gunmen at a checkpoint and held for ten days in a specially constructed concrete box under one of the smuggler's homes; their imprisonment only ended when they fought their way out. The kidnappers initially claimed to be *shabiha*—and in an elaborate charade pretended to shoot the Syrian driver who'd brought them in—but it quickly became clear that this was a criminal gang flying the flag of the Free Syrian Army and working closely with Islamic extremists. In an odd way, Wood told me, "their cover story was closer to the reality, because these were people who'd always done business with the regime."

Stories even surfaced of fixers, working with rebel kidnappers, trying to lure journalists into Northern Syria on the
promise of juicy stories. A month after Paul Wood was kidnapped a French-American photographer called Jonathan
Alpeyrie was betrayed by his fixer soon after he crossed the
Lebanese border. After three months and several mock executions, he was released; but only, he told me, after $450,000 was
paid via pro-regime middlemen to his Islamist kidnappers. In
the same month and the same general area Domenico Quirico,
an Italian reporter, along with a Belgian teacher, Pierre Piccinin da Prata, were speeding away from the city of al-Qusayr
when they were extracted at gunpoint by men claiming to be
with the Syrian regime. It was another "fool's kidnapping"—
their kidnappers were working closely with their rebel mind-
ers and had staged the whole thing. Over the following five
months they'd be passed around three different rebel militias
on a journey first south to the suburbs of Damascus and then
back through the length of Northern Syria before arriving in
Turkey. "We were luggage," da Prata told me. "Just merchandise. The bandits only tried to keep us alive."

The problem was how to make the deal. Al-Qusayr was soon
surrounded by the Syrian army and their allies Hezbollah, with
no way in or out. With fierce fighting and shelling all around,
the two men were sent for safe keeping to a host of different
Islamist groups, including al-Qaeda. Two months after they'd
been taken following a hair-raising forty-eight-hour dash across
country, their kidnappers broke through Syrian army lines and
delivered the hostages to another rebel brigade. In the chaos da
Prata persuaded a fighter to let him phone home; it was the first
time he'd been able to tell his family he was still alive.

It was also the moment at which negotiations for their release began. Ammar Boka'i, the bearded, charismatic rebel commander who'd taken over their custody, was kindly enough. Before the war Boka'i had been a housepainter; his father, he told one of his hostages, was a Sufi sheikh who could even charm snakes. As the Syrian revolt moved from street protests to street fighting, he'd risen fast through the ranks of the Free Syrian Army's Farouq Brigade, which had initially grown up to protect anti-regime demonstrations in Homs. The Farouq was popular and powerful; it liked smuggling foreign journalists into rebel-held neighborhoods, and foreign journalists liked it in return. After the rebels drew back from Homs in February 2012, however, things turned bad. Resources had always been tight, but now some complained that the Farouq wasn't doing its fair share of their fighting, and was intimidating those who spoke up to complain. Shaken by a series of scandals, the Farouq shed fighters and shattered into different groups. The rump that remained leaned more heavily on smuggling and illicit trading to make money, and the Farouq lost ground to Islamist groups who came to lead the insurgency.

Boka'i told Quirico and da Prata that middlemen had already being employed to open up a dialogue with the Italian authorities, and that they would be released very soon. "You were kidnapped by al-Qaeda," he told them, "but we are here to protect you and to try and save you." It was another charade: they were only a few kilometers from the Lebanese border, and could have been allowed to go back there at any time. Boka'i had become one of the snakes.

Ammar Boka'i handled the negotiations like a consummate professional; it was he who asked the proof of life questions required by the middlemen, and he who took control of the horse-trading that rumbled on for the next three months. Da Prata had reason to think that he opened the bidding with the Italian authorities at ten million dollars; the Belgian government, to his irritation, refused to pay. Da Prata also remembers another man, a shisha-smoking, constantly-eating whirlwind of activity called Mahmoud, who served as one of Boka'i's deputies and was always surrounded by a phalanx of armed men. "He was the banker and the money man; his job was to organize the budget. He would arrive with plastic bags bulging with money, dollars as well as Syrian lira." One evening bricks of hundred-dollar bills were piled high on the table; at least some of it, thinks da Prata, was counterfeit. Like Boka'i, Mahmoud generally treated the men well, bringing them food and even including them in the joke but also mocking them. "You want money," he'd say; "I have lots of money."

Realizing that the change in their guard didn't suggest an imminent release the two men began to panic, but Mahmoud did his best to put them at their ease. "Don't worry," he said, "we are just trying to get some money from your governments, after which you can go back to your countries. Did you hear about the Russian journalist who was kidnapped some months back? We did it. She stayed in my house in al-Qusayr, and then she went back to Russia. There was a ransom. She even had time to learn Arabic."

It was true. The Russian was Anhar Kochneva, a Ukrainian blogger who worked closely with Russian media in Syria and who'd been kidnapped by exactly the same people the previous October. Like Quirico and da Prata, she'd been held for five months and moved around several times, and just like them her ordeal began in al-Qusayr. In Kochneva's case, however, the target was the car. The wallets of the Free Syrian Army's foreign supporters had never quite matched their rhetoric, and an Audi A8 was a coveted vehicle. When they drove it back to their base, remembers a former member of the Farouq who was there the day Kochneva was brought in, one young rebel couldn't wait to tell the man in charge. "Look!" he shouted. "I brought you a car." But the boss was confused: "Who is the girl in the back?" The next day the calls began to flood in. One was from Syria's feared General Intelligence Directorate, another came direct from the Presidential Palace. The caller, according to the Farouq fighter, said: "We want this girl—we can give you whatever you want. They didn't even mention the other two. So we knew she was a big deal."

The news that a Russian had been caught lifted morale among the rebels, who were then struggling to lift a siege of their outposts in Homs; in the excitement some convinced themselves Kochneva was KGB, others that Putin's own office was involved in the operation to get her back. There was no evidence for any of it. All the same, proof of life questions arrived from the Syrian authorities and were duly answered; one asked for the name of the travel agency for which she worked, another for the name of her dog. A delegation was rustled up to see Boka'i, who'd since arrived and taken Kochneva away, demanding that she be bartered not for money but in return for relief of the besieged areas or for hundreds of rebel prisoners. Boka'i said that he'd have to talk to his boss, the overall leader of the Farouq, but returned the following day and said, "I've slaughtered her." No one believed him, and tensions began to rise.

After ten days, her driver was released for twenty thousand dollars, but the kidnappers were much more excited by Kochneva. Under duress, she was forced to record videos in which she admitted to being a military translator for Russian officers. Her captors demanded fifty million dollars for her release.

When I spoke to Kochneva after she had been freed she was still in Damascus—and still fuming about her 153 days as a hostage of serial kidnappers. "Tens of thousands of people have been kidnapped in Syria, mostly the Syrians. But there are many people for whom no one will pay. They are demanding unrealistic money for foreigners, and to justify this they call them spies or military advisers. At first they only kidnapped those who supported the Syrian regime; now, with their funds drying up, they are taking even foreigners who are loyal to their cause." She had a point. While the international media seemed most exercised by the use of chemical weapons in the conflict, the Syrians I met cared much more about being kidnapped and their families threatened or hounded for money—for many it was one of their worst fears. Huge numbers of ordinary Syrians were being kidnapped, with no one to pay a ransom or even investigate who might be responsible. While some were whisked away by forces loyal to the regime, a good many were taken by one of the many rival militias that have grown up on the other side. As whole areas of the country fell into chaos and criminality, kidnapping became a weapon and a crucial source of finance for the warring parties.

On the phone, Kochneva sounded bitter; amid all the interest in glory-hunting foreign journalists, cases like hers had received scant attention. Her time in captivity, in a cold room with a broken window, had taken a toll on her health; she didn't even have enough money to go back to Moscow and see her daughter, or visit her doctor regularly. No one had done anything to help her. Like da Prata, she well remembered both Boka'i and Mahmoud. Boka'i had certainly led the negotiations for her release, but Kochneva insisted that no money had changed hands. She'd simply escaped, walking for fifteen kilometers until she arrived at government territory. "Do you not think that someone who has millions of dollars to pay for a blogger could afford to fill her fridge or buy her a pill?" she told me. "Nobody paid a kopek."

When ransoms *were* paid, however, the victims were often the last to know. Da Prata, for example, had no idea how much was handed over to secure his and Quirico's release until an article in a Dutch newspaper put the figure at four million dollars. In an interview on the Syrian–Turkish border the week after they were set free, I spoke to a high-ranking local rebel called Wasseem, whose figures were more precise. The ransom, according to Wasseem, was nearly five million dollars, four million of which was paid by the Italian authorities; Boka'i received $1.5 million, while the original kidnapper took two million and the rest went to middlemen.

Wasseem didn't believe that Boka'i could have been behind the initial abduction, but was certain that he'd been happy to profit from the crime. The kidnapper had simply "gone to the expert." Given Mahmoud's admission to da Prata and the behavior of both the rebels and the regime at the time, it seems very likely that a deal was behind Kochneva's release too. The last place she was kept, Wasseem and his colleagues claimed, was far away from government-held territory. In any case, she was well guarded, and in that part of rural, conservative Syria it would have been impossible for a woman to walk such a distance without being noticed. "The regime and the Farouq have the same secret," said Wasseem. "Neither wants to make it public."

Whatever the truth of how Kochneva won her freedom, it wouldn't be the first time that a lucky escape from Syrian kidnappers would engender wholesale suspicion. In July 2013 an unknown group of gunmen burst into a media office in Idlib and dragged off a Polish photographer called Marcin Suder. A Syrian friend of his who tried to protect him was badly beaten; the next day the kidnappers emailed him an apology. "We wanted the journalist," they said, "and we will keep him for a ransom." Three months later he re-appeared in Turkey. The Polish Foreign Ministry announced that Suder had escaped, but no one I've spoken to, including his Syrian friend and a member of the security team working to get him out, believed it; given his location inside Syria and the determination of his kidnappers, everyone with any knowledge of the area assumed that money must have been paid to secure his release. But no one really knew.[2] This lack of transparency would become one of the thorniest problems for the families of foreign hostages held in Syria. Since none of the parties to any ransom negotiation had any incentive to talk, and information was often hidden at the request of both sides, no one got to find out who was kidnapping whom and what could be done—and what was being handed over to secure the release of foreign hostages.

---

2. Despite repeated attempts to contact him over a year, Marcin Suder refused my requests for an interview about the circumstances of his release. But in an email he insisted that he had escaped, and that he was not able to confirm who had abducted him. However, whoever kidnapped Suder was very unlikely to be from ISIS; none of the Islamic State hostages appear to have met Suder at any point in their captivity.

When da Prata arrived at the Turkish border after his release, an Italian secret service agent took him aside and whispered that he "was very lucky to have been traveling with an Italian"; the lesson that the Italians generally pay would not have been lost on Syrian kidnappers either. Kidnapping for ransom is relatively easy to solve if a friendly government or business-man can be found to stump up the cash. It was Quirico and da Prata's good fortune, sniffed another rebel I spoke to, to be sold "like a packet of cigarettes" to someone who appreciated their financial value.

Starting in Homs in February 2012, the Syrian army pounded parts of the country's biggest cities with rockets, air strikes and barrel bombs. The aim seems to have been to drain the sea in which the armed opposition swam, but the result was to annihilate the social fabric and leave millions of Syrians with little to lose. It was the perfect breeding ground for revenge cults like the al-Qaeda affiliate Jabhat al-Nusra, which grew out of militant Islamism and quickly won respect for its fight-ing prowess.

When some influential Egyptian clerics announced it the duty of every Sunni Muslim to wage war on the Syrian regime, the country became a magnet for foreign fighters, or *muha-jireen*, like those who would pick up John Cantlie and Jeroen Oerlemans. A combination of battle-hardened Islamists and furiously devout novices, they arrived in such numbers and with such unusual garb and paraphernalia that parts of North-ern Syria began to resemble a jihadi Disneyland. In need of the assistance, local rebels turned a blind eye to their puritanical excesses, and welcomed their support.

The strain of militant Islamism was there in Syria's insurgency from the beginning, obvious to anyone who cared to look. Their motives for kidnapping foreigners were, however, more ambiguous. Two American journalists who'd gone missing in different areas of Northern Syria in late 2012 had quietly been abducted and taken to the same prison in Aleppo. One, a photographer called Matt Schrier, would show up in southern Turkey the following summer with a tale of almost gothic depravity. He'd just escaped, he told the *New York Times*, from a brutal network of underground prisons run mostly by Jabhat al-Nusra; his jailers had tortured him, coaxed him into making taped confessions admitting he worked for the CIA, even drained his bank account and sent emails to his family in his name.

The wealthier factions, including Nusra, often didn't kidnap for money but as ammunition for upcoming hostage exchanges; most of the deals brokered between the Syrian regime and rebel forces turned on the exchange of prisoners. In this giddy internal market someone might be kidnapped for one reason and then sold on to another group for an entirely different purpose. Matt Schrier told me that a fellow prisoner, a well-connected Syrian, had been sold by the Free Syrian Army to his kidnappers for eighty thousand dollars; in turn, Nusra was looking to use him in a prisoner swap with the Syrian regime.

For much of his seven months of captivity, Schrier's cellmate was the other kidnapped American, Theo Padnos. Padnos had been encouraged into Syria in the autumn of 2012 by a group of young rebels, and then promptly beaten and handed over to Jabhat al-Nusra as a suspected spy. It was a common enough accusation. Almost every journalist I've ever met in Syria has been accused of being a spook.

So had Austin Tice. When his Free Syrian Army friends at the Turkish border found none of his journalism online, but lots of information about his background in the Marines, two of them told me, they'd drawn the conclusion that Tice was an American agent. "The CIA or the Pentagon," shrugged one. It was wishful thinking at a time when the Free Syrian Army was desperately trying to secure foreign military support, and Tice was aware of it; in one of the tweets he left behind he notes that "A lot of ppl assume I'm CIA, in a sort of sad, 'America DOES care!' kind of way." But he was no fool. Shortly before Tice went missing, one of his editors told me, he'd been approached via the internet by someone in the British Embassy in Lebanon, presumably an intelligence officer—after taking advice from the editor he refused to take the conversation any further.

While there are undoubtedly journalists with intelligence connections working in war zones—after all, "journalism makes great cover," as one security expert told me—the regularity with which the accusation was levelled at the foreign media in Syria rendered it meaningless. While one Islamist rebel commander I'd been in touch with for over a year assured me that the Free Syrian Army had very good reason to interrogate embedded foreign journalists—"Some of them are working with the regime"—Paul Wood, weary of the spy allegation, dismissed it as a morale-booster and a way of driving up ransoms. "The spy thing is instinctive anywhere in the Arab world. You want to say, you fucking idiot, you've got one donkey and a Kalashnikov, why would I be spying on you?"

To Syria's growing population of radical Islamists, however, the assumption was that *every* foreigner was a spy. Taking too close an interest in European jihadis would be grounds enough for detention; so would an American passport, or even one from a European country that supported the U.S. Balint Szlanko, one of the two Eastern European freelancers who'd shared their roof in Northern Syria with Jim Foley in July 2012, was briefly arrested by an Islamist militia in Aleppo in the following months; the other, an Albanian Kosovar photographer called Vedat Zhymshiti, was one of the few to be kidnapped twice. On the second occasion he was dolefully informed that since he came from a pro-American country he was CIA and deserved to be beheaded. Handcuffed to a chair in front of a yelling, sword-wielding Somali American, he was only saved by the intervention of friendly rebels who stormed the building and shot dead his kidnappers.

Regime agents posing as Islamists, rebels affecting to be *shabiha*—digging for information on the whereabouts of missing journalists was like wading through quicksand. For those of us who were following the story at the time, it was clear that they were becoming pawns in a paranoid new game in which the kidnappers were often not who they seemed, and had convinced themselves that their victims weren't either. Nervous editors and news producers were worried that journalists were now legitimate targets in Syria, but it was worse than that. It was becoming the hunting season.

CHAPTER TWO

Come with Us, It Will Only Take Five Minutes...

When the two Western journalists went missing on the afternoon of November 22, 2012, a skinny, street-smart Syrian taxi driver would be the first to come under suspicion—which was odd, he thought, because they'd come to him and not the other way around. His only crime was to have parked his taxi outside a Binnish internet café when Mustafa had poked his head around the door and told him: *These two journalists need to go to the Turkish border, pronto, and our usual ride has let us down.*

Abdulkader was happy to help. A fare to the border with two foreign guests was better than he was hoping for that day; foreigners paid generous tips. In any case, he recognized the journalists; he didn't know them well enough to call them friends, but he'd seen them around in the city they had made their headquarters. Even apart from the presence of their likable local fixer Mustafa, the location of Binnish in a staunch rebel bastion of Northern Syria made it an excellent forward operating base. Shut your eyes to the Soviet-style breezeblock architecture and the place had a beauty about it too. Situated on a hill with magnificent views topped by two striking mosques, one of which dated from the colonial era, Binnish was, like much of the surrounding province of Idlib, famous for its olives. Even now, amid rolling, wild vegetation and sites of rugged archeological beauty, the whole area resembled a kind of unspoiled, antiquarian golf course—a world away from the arid, dusty stereotype of Arabia.

It helped that the living was cheap, and that the locals had turned hospitality into an art form. Starved of any relationship with the outside world by the sclerotic, ever-watchful regime of President Bashar al-Assad, most Binnishis saw foreigners as tantalizing delicacies. Since the Syrian revolt had turned into an armed insurgency, Binnish had fought its way out of the control of the Syrian regime and into the hands of a motley parade of rebel groups. Life wasn't perfect—constantly shifting groups of armed men patrolled the streets—but the locals who hadn't fled the fighting mostly preferred it. A little freedom, they reasoned, was a lot better than none at all.

The mood in the taxi was light, horseplay and ribaldry going back and forth. Abdulkader, laid-back but eager to please, didn't speak any English and didn't know his new companions' names, but found them very funny anyway. One was an American called Jim Foley; the other beside him on the backseat was a Brit, John Cantlie. Mustafa sat in the front, occasionally craning his neck around to share in the jokes. All three needed to let off a little steam. Spending time in a war zone seriously tests the nerves, but heading in the other direction, body parts still intact and with some great material in the can, there's no feeling like it—every war reporter knows that it's better than sex. It's even more of a rush if you're freelance, working to a tight budget and without a carful of expensive knuckleheads, otherwise known as a security team, to cover you if anything goes wrong.

Better still when you're in the company of good friends. For the past three weeks, broken up by occasional breathers on the Turkish side of the border, the three had risked their lives to bring back the stories that the lumbering big media was too timid, or too tight-fisted, to go anywhere near. With the Syrian air force conducting daily raids, Northern Syria was so dangerous that most staff journalists went in and out for a few days at a time, often surrounded by producers and a security detail. Not Cantlie and Foley. Foley had spent much of the last eight months like this, sneaking in and out for two-week stretches at a time; Cantlie had been around less, but was getting used to the drill. The long-haul, down-at-heel approach suited them both; at its best, it was more authentic, with richer dividends to be had by living with ordinary people.

It was living among the people that had got Foley into this business in the first place. He was relatively new to war reporting—he'd worked for a non-profit teaching literature to kids in run-down neighborhoods back home in America before becoming a journalist—but had won his spurs as a reporter on the U.S army newspaper *Stars and Stripes*, and had spent time on military bases in Iraq and Afghanistan. Being fed and watered by a protective phalanx of American troops was a walk in the park compared to fending for yourself in Syria, where no one knew what the hell was going on, but

Foley liked to think it suited him better. Affable and given to calling even colleagues he barely knew "sister" or "brother," Foley had none of the huckster machismo of some war-zone junkies. He'd made friends quickly, and earned respect for his ability to let video tell a story. His lantern-jawed, movie-star looks made him stand out too, along with deep-set, haunted-looking eyes.

Maybe he was haunted. Eighteen months earlier, while riding with three fellow journalists in rebel-held Libya, he'd been arrested and held for six weeks by the Gaddafi regime. One of the four, a South African photographer called Anton Hammerl, had been shot and his body left in the desert. The experience of not being able to save a badly wounded colleague, of leaving him to die in the dust, had hit Foley hard; so much so that he'd set up a fund to help Hammerl's family. After he'd come back he'd written an article for Marquette, the private Jesuit University where he'd studied fifteen years previously, about how praying the rosary along with his female colleague had helped him get through his time in captivity.

After his kidnapping in Libya, Foley was persuaded to stay home and take a desk job, but he soon grew restless. He wanted to get back to reporting war, and Syria was where the story was headed. Foley was a freelancer, and luckier than most—he sent much of his stuff to a maverick Boston start-up called *Global-Post* which specialized in covering the parts of the world that big media couldn't get into or didn't want to touch—and then selling it back to them for money. But there was no way around it: the freelance life had certain hazards that went along with it. In a *Newsweek* article published in October 2012, Foley spoke candidly about the pressures, the slim rewards and the temptation to go the risky extra mile. "The idea was to go past where the majority would go, get better stuff because no one else was there," he said. "It's the freelancer's conundrum taking bigger risks to beat staffers. I think it's just basic laws of competition; you need to have something the staffers don't, but in a conflict zone that means you take bigger risks: go in sooner, stay longer, go closer."

Foley and Cantlie were both in early middle age, but still had a boyish thirst for adventure. And like almost all freelancers in the area, they were instinctively on the side of the rebels in these new Arab awakenings. Unlike all the *arrivistes*, they'd been there from the beginning. Last year they'd been together in Libya, inching along in an advance guard of rebels as they moved on the dangerous city of Sirte. Now they were in a different country, doing much the same thing.

Tall and buff with the bearing of a military man on the brink of insubordination, Cantlie's reputation for wily bravado made Foley look cautious, which was saying something. Cantlie, too, had lived many lives before war-zone journalism; he was a motorcycling nut and had once worked as a video-game tester. He hailed from a buccaneering British colonial family; his great grandfather Sir James had once led a media campaign to the life of the Chinese revolutionary Sun Yat-sen. On one occasion Cantlie had accompanied the two British princes William and Harry on a grueling eight-day, sixteen-hundred-kilometer cycling trek through Africa that sold itself as a charity ride but looked more like an endurance test. He was also given to feats of Flashman-like derring-do, and had a reputation for going gladly to the places other journalists couldn't reach. It bordered on recklessness, but it could reap rich rewards. Earlier in 2012, in the city of Saraqeb, Cantlie, along with Foley and Mustafa, had found himself in the middle of a sudden and very dangerous regime assault. Most photographers would have charged in the other direction, but Cantlie had stood his ground, staring down the barrel of an advancing Soviet T-72 tank to get the shot. It was worth it; the picture, along with Foley's video, was published around the world.

John Cantlie had also been kidnapped, of course, six months previously and only a stone's throw from the very same Bab al-Hawa border crossing where they were now headed. That hair-raising week he'd spent in the custody of British jihadis was the main reason he'd come back. He'd written a lengthy article about the experience for the *Sunday Times*, and agreed to a number of TV interviews. Interest picked up further when one of the jihadis he'd identified, Shajul Islam, a young doctor from east London, returned to the UK and was promptly arrested. Here at last was a story about Syria that Western audiences could identify with, and the British and international media loved it. Now he'd come back to do it properly, this time as a journalist with a camera rather than as a hostage, creating the definitive account of how European Islamists were beginning to muscle in on someone's else civil war.

In the previous two weeks he'd got some great footage; it was all safely on his computer. With Mustafa in tow he'd actually gone back to the jihadi training facility where he'd been held; its leader had recently been assassinated by mainstream rebels affiliated to the Free Syrian Army, and the rest had scattered. Cantlie had even found his own business card and photo

ID lying in the mud. This was a story only he could tell, and he had high hopes of selling it when he returned.

Now it was time for them to leave. The plan was to drive the forty kilometers to the Turkish border, leaving the journalists to go onward while Mustafa returned to Binnish with Abdulkader. First of all, however, they'd need to go to Mustafa's house to fetch their equipment, computers and video cameras that were almost as heavy as they were.

While the journalists collected their stuff Abdulkader waited outside. When they returned to the taxi, Mustafa announced he'd left his mobile phone in the internet café where he'd picked the journalists up, which meant everyone going all the way back so he could fetch it. They'd been in the café for over an hour; the journalists had wanted to file some copy and chat with friends on Skype and email. Cantlie, who planned to return home to London immediately, wrote a brief note to his partner: "Be home soon. See you in a few hours." Foley had been exchanging messages with his younger sister Katie; back home it was Thanksgiving and everyone wanted to wish him a good one, but he'd been so busy with everything that the date had slipped his mind. He'd also pinged Nicole Tung, his photographer friend who was waiting for him across the border, and who often came with him into Syria; if it hadn't been for a broken camera she'd have been on this trip too. He and Nicole began brainstorming an itinerary for a new trip back inside Syria; other than that he'd just wanted to tell her that all was good and that he'd see her in Turkey very soon. "It was a normal conversation," she told me. "There was nothing untoward."

*   *   *

Nobody starts out wanting to be a fixer for foreign journalists—Mustafa wanted to be a photographer—but the money and the company were good, and it was an exciting new connection to the outside world. Mustafa was in his mid-twenties, much younger than the other two men. With long, rock-star hair and trendy, angular glasses, he looked far cooler than almost anyone living in the middle of a civil war. It was one of the reasons the journalists took to him so quickly; that, his serviceable English and his easy laughter, even if much of it was a nervous tic. Mustafa had started out naïve and ended up heartbroken. His whole family had thrown in their lot with the rebels, and had its soul ripped out by the growing fallout from the civil war. His young niece would be killed in a regime air strike; for a long time her face would feature where his should have been on his Facebook profile.

But for Mustafa, journalists weren't part of the problem. Far from making his lot worse, he considered them a potential way out. Most of the time he thought of James and John not as two individuals but as an inseparable pair—"J&J," he called them. He'd spent a good deal of time with them now, and counted them as benefactors as well as employers.

The relationship wasn't perfect. One time Mustafa had complained to an acquaintance that Foley hadn't given any money to the family they'd stayed with—Mustafa liked to see the people around him treated well, and foreigners usually had more money, but that was freelancers for you. But J&J had both patiently coached Mustafa in photography. His shots—including one taken within nodding distance of a Syrian regime fighter pilot flying low on a bombing raid—had been good enough to be published by some of the biggest news agencies in the world.

Though he agreed to help them, Mustafa did grumble about the merits of making another story of Cantlie's kidnapping. Of more serious concern were Cantlie's attempts at chumminess with foreign jihadis. It wasn't clear what he was trying to prove and, given what had happened the last time, it was a clear risk to their security. Just two weeks before, on a tour of rebel-held Aleppo, Mustafa remembered him wandering over to a huddle of European jihadis and trying to draw them into a conversation. They'd spoken very good English, but the small talk hadn't lasted long. "Do know the British guy?" one asked. "You know, the journalist who was kidnapped and then put our doctor in prison." They knew everything about his story. "Oh yeah that guy," he'd dissembled frantically. "I heard about this story, but I don't know him." Then Cantlie had retraced his steps and announced that all of them needed to leave immediately. His face was pale as anything—it was the first time Mustafa had ever seen him afraid—but Mustafa had begged him not to do anything else that put them under suspicion; so, instead of hot-footing it away, they'd ambled around idly and then left as soon as seemed decent. "Do you think I'm in danger right now?" Cantlie had asked on their way out, and Mustafa had almost thumped him. "Yes, you are. Because of your mouth. Never ever ask them questions, and don't put your camera on them: they will hurt you."

A little more diplomatically, Foley was trying to talk Cantlie down, to make sure he was aware of the risks. "John, you must be careful, they don't love us," Mustafa remembers him saying. "They are thinking that we are CIA, that we are spies. They don't want us to be in Syria." The experience seemed to have shaken Cantlie up; not long afterward he'd thought to email Jeroen Oerlemans, the Dutch journalist who'd been kidnapped with him in July, to tell him the news.

To some, Cantlie's run-in with European jihadis in Aleppo might have seemed like a good story, but to Mustafa it was unforgivable. "Every time he was making trouble for me and James." The latest incident had happened in the internet café just before they'd hailed Abdulkader's taxi. A foreign jihadi, who had the appearance of a Gulf Arab, had strolled into the café wearing a beret and Cantlie, ever friendly to enigmatic strangers, had tried for a joke. "Hey, Che Guevara!" he'd called, but not only did the guy not reply, he'd given all of them the evil eye. After just one or two minutes at the computer terminal the jihadi had paid the owner and left. Foley had shouted at Cantlie and told him to shut up. For Mustafa it was another red flag, a sign that they were becoming too comfortable for their own good.

Mustafa fetched his phone from the internet café—it was still there—and they set off again, this time on their way to the border. The taxi ride would take about forty-five minutes, and would have been even quicker but for an onerous but necessary detour. The point was to avoid the nearby Shia village of Fua, which was still a regime stronghold and which they couldn't go near for fear of being arrested, kidnapped or worse. The two settlements, Binnish and Fua, neatly told the tragic story of Syria's revolution as it spiraled out of control in rural areas over the previous twelve months. Rebel-held Binnish and regime holdout Fua run right up against each other, and before the uprising relations were broadly harmonious.

Many young people from Binnish had friends in Fua and vice versa. But demonstrations against the regime in Sunni Binnish weren't matched by those in Shia Fua, and gangs of *shabiha* grew up in the latter to enforce the regime's rule. Community life gave way to daily clashes, sandbagged checkpoints, punishing air strikes and a vicious cycle of kidnapping and counter-kidnapping. Most of the civilians left.

Abdulkader, however, had stayed put. Taxi driving, along with fixing for foreign journalists, was one of the few jobs still open to Syrians that didn't involve carrying a gun. As a driver he prided himself on knowing the way around, the byways and the safe routes, which roads to avoid for fear of hostile gunmen or random shelling. One lazy wrong turn or impatient short-cut could make the difference between kidnapping or worse, either for him or for his fare.

For some time now, the only route to the border had been to circle around Fua to the east via Taftanaz, a town then firmly in rebel hands. On the way down the Old Aleppo Road, Fua safely in the distance to their left, the first village they passed was Toum, another rebel redoubt and no threat to people like them. As he always did now, Abdulkader sped up. The Syrian army was on the defensive in the area but remained in control of the local military airport, and snipers in its outbuildings had been known to take pot shots at passing cars. It was shortly after he took his foot off the accelerator that he noticed a large Hyundai speeding very quickly up behind them. "There are vans like this for people and vans for goods. This was a goods vehicle," Abdulkader said. Just as they approached the north-western entrance to Taftanaz, and as he was about to bear left, the Hyundai drew level with his taxi and the driver rolled his window down, gesturing at him to pull over. Abdulkader slowed down a little more, thinking that the driver might need some help, but the Hyundai took the opportunity to overtake him and brake suddenly, forcing both vehicles to grind to a halt.

What happened next is a series of painful blurs. Three armed men launched themselves from the doors of the Hyundai, shooting wildly in the air. One was wearing a mask, while the others were wearing keffiyehs to obscure their faces. The men were shouting at everyone to get out of the car, but Mustafa and the journalists were pleading with Abdulkader not to open the door. It was too late for that. The journalists were hauled outside and screamed at in Arabic to get "down, down" on the ground. Abdulkader had no idea who these men were or what they wanted with the journalists, and concluded that honesty might be the best policy: "I am just a driver, I don't know these men." One of the attackers tried to speak to Foley and Cantlie in Arabic, and when that failed they dragged Mustafa out of the car to get him to translate. Mustafa was forced to tie up the journalists with keffiyehs. After that, the men put both the journalists and their equipment in the back of the goods vehicle.

It was all over in a few minutes. The only thing Abdulkader was sure about was that this was a planned operation. "They were on a mission, it was not by chance." Mustafa was beside himself, frantically talking up his rebel connections and offering to accompany the men to wherever they were going. None of it worked. Just before they drove off, Mustafa remembers the kidnappers striking a note of cryptic reassurance: "We just want to ask these men one question. Then, I swear to God, we will bring them back in five minutes."

After Mustafa raised the alarm among friends of Foley and Cantlie, communications hell broke loose. Everyone was phoning and emailing everyone else—tapping contacts for leads, calling in favors from friendly rebel commanders, tipping off anyone who needed to know. Nicole Tung, waiting on the other side of the border, was one of the first to find out, and immediately leaned on everyone she knew to try to help. Plenty of others stepped up too; in the tight circle of jobbing journalists and photographers who worked Northern Syria, Jim Foley was a familiar face. *GlobalPost* also acted quickly. Within days its insurers had kidnap investigators on the ground in Turkey, talking to anyone who might be able to help. They'd been supplied at considerable expense by the security firm Kroll, and Mustafa was one of the first people they spoke to. A few weeks later Abdulkader met the investigators, but only in extreme haste as he fled Syria—he'd had enough of living in fear of his life, and decided to take his family to Lebanon.

Long before the Syrian conflict, professional kidnap and ransom investigators were getting plenty of work. After the Cold War, the taking of hostages for political goals seemed like the relic of a bygone age. In the years since, however, a new kind of kidnapping enterprise had emerged: the taking of hostages for the purposes of extorting money from businesses, organizations and insurers rather than governments.

The industry was often aided by a region's chaos and instabil-
ity, but their actions were about profit not politics. The biggest
growth came from Latin America and parts of Africa, where
the abduction of high-value targets such as businessmen and
insured foreign workers was relatively easy money. Growing
alongside it was a lucrative new sector of the private security
industry: K&R. Commercial kidnap and ransom insurance,
in the fractured, post-Cold War terrain of failed states and
impoverished armies, and buoyed up by the risks of sending
high-value employees overseas, has found an eager market.
Everything about it is hush-hush. The world's most respected
K&R outfits are tiny, boutique companies you will never have
heard of.

There are sound reasons to keep things under wraps. Since
kidnap investigations occur in real time, while the crime is still
happening, one false move can make things worse. Courting
publicity puts immediate pressure on governments or families to negotiate, which can drive up the price of a release. K&R
is also just about the only kind of insurance cover for which
a beneficiary's knowledge of the existence of their policy is
enough to invalidate it; if word got out that anyone was definitely insured, they'd become an immediate target. The industry also requires investigators to work out who's holding the
hostage, bean-counters to keep an eye on the insurance mar-
kets, middlemen to tout the hostage around and set up the
deal, extraction guys to wade in and attempt a rescue if things
look like they might turn bad, insurance companies or families to foot the bill—and kidnappers, without whom everyone
else would be out of a job.

Not everyone is convinced that it works. One K&R professional who has worked on Syria cases was candid about the problems thrown up by the existence of his own profession: "What this industry has created is a need for a constant drip, drip, drip of intelligence every week. It preys on people's worst fears: the worst thing is a lack of news. If you went missing I could figure out a good way to drip you information over a year. But the point is not to find information but to solve the problem. How do you monetize the contract for sitting and waiting? It's not a good model." Another problem with commercial agencies working for insurance money, the former MI6 officer Alastair Crooke told me, is that they want to get in and out quickly—to throw money at the problem. "Once people get it into their head that foreigners have insurance and these security contractors will arrive, the effect is to create a market. People begin to smell money—do you want to buy a hostage? We had that all the time when I was dealing with hostage cases. And you get overwhelmed with disinformation."

Even if you do get hold of the right people, says Crooke, too often the result is a tantalizing trail of information designed to wring the most money from the deal. "They'll throw out a few enticing nuggets, and then say, 'OK, if you want more, like a proof of life, this is what it's going to cost you.' Then you're going to be taken for further series of demands to drive up the ransom. The small fish don't expect to get the big money; they don't have the hostage. But they're easy prey for a few hundred dollars for a commercial firm. People learn the art of telling tall stories. The important thing is to open up trustworthy lines of communication, to be very skeptical, asking 'Who is saying this? What is his motive?' But it's more expensive. We spent huge sums precisely because we didn't pay ransom; it's much more costly."

Bob Baer, a former CIA case officer in the Middle East, sighed at the litany of faces who must now be showing up at Syria's Turkish border trying to broker deals; he reckoned he might know a few of them from his days in Beirut. "There's this huge swindle which starts when people go missing—a whole mini-industry based on lies and fraud. Governments are vulnerable too. People claim to know shit; you hear the most fantastic stories. I've spent more money than you'd care to know about, CIA money, following these leads."

The first I heard about the kidnapping of Jim Foley and John Cantlie was about six weeks after it happened, from Yasser, the opposition activist I'd spent time with in Damascus a year earlier. Now in exile, he was based at the Turkish border and claimed to be working with the Free Syrian Army. In our phone call, Yasser told me that he and his colleagues were still investigating, but they believed that the two journalists had been driven to Fua by pro-regime *shabiha* and then whisked hundreds of kilometers south to Damascus.

The best evidence for this theory seemed to be the pattern of kidnappings in a nearby area. Three weeks after Foley and Cantlie went missing, the NBC correspondent Richard Engel and his entire team were nabbed near the same border crossing by suspected pro-regime paramilitaries; they surfaced five days later, following the making of a kidnap video, a shoot-out and their rescue by an Islamist rebel group. Some of the team hired by Kroll to work on the Foley case were allowed to speak to some of the rescued NBC team, and to have access to the notes which followed their initial debriefing—all of which suggested that they'd been taken by pro-regime *shabiha*.

Other circumstantial evidence in their case also pointed subtly in the direction of the Syrian regime. At that time, most journalists who'd been abducted by rebel groups had been interrogated for a few days to make sure they weren't spies and then sent on their way with a stiff warning. If Foley and Cantlie had fallen into the hands of a rebel brigade hungry for money the families would surely have received a ransom demand, but none had been forthcoming. Then there was the uncharacteristic lack of chatter. Foley's reporter friends had good relationships with many of the rebel brigades; a good few of them had been traveling under their protection. In the ready market for information that had grown up in Syria, the kidnapping of two Western journalists by any significant rebel faction would be news—it would be expected to travel fast, and to leak. Not long after the kidnapping, friends of the pair had even interrupted a conference of rebel commanders in Turkey to have them ring around everyone they knew in the area regarding the men's whereabouts. Everything came back empty—no one had them.

By May 2013, six months after the kidnapping and amid mounting pressure for results, *GlobalPost* made up its mind. "With a very high degree of confidence," its CEO and Foley's editor Phil Balboni said in a speech which was subsequently reported in *GlobalPost*, "we now believe that Jim was most likely abducted by a pro-regime militia group and subsequently turned over to Syrian government forces." The organization had "obtained multiple independent reports from very credible confidential sources," and the detail was impressive. Foley, it was reckoned, was being held in a Damascus prison facility run by the Syrian Air Force Intelligence, the most feared fief within the security state. Balboni's speech included one final explosive detail: "It is likely Jim is being held with one or more Western journalists, including most likely at least one other American." The American, everyone assumed, was Austin Tice.

It was bombshell information, but raised many more questions than it answered. To almost every journalist on the ground along the Turkish–Syrian border, the theory that Jim Foley and John Cantlie had been abducted by regime *shabiha* didn't make sense. Foley was traveling from Binnish, a rebel stronghold, en route to the rebel-held border crossing at Bab al-Hawa; the whole point of the circuitous route was to avoid the regime-held outpost of Fua and the attentions of *shabiha*. Six months earlier Taftanaz would have been accessible to regime forces, but now everyone who'd been there reported that it was thick with wild-eyed foreign jihadis and the military airport was under siege; two months on, the airport itself would fall to the rebels. Nor did the regime theory seem to pay full heed to the eyewitnesses. Mustafa had always been clear that this couldn't have been the work of forces loyal to the Syrian regime. It was especially puzzling to Nicole Tung because, in the immediate aftermath of the kidnap, there'd been no question at all of regime involvement. As she recalled, "There was no mention of government paramilitaries at that stage."

The doubters included a British journalist who definitely had been arrested by forces loyal to the Syrian regime, in the same area and three weeks before Jim Foley and John Cantlie went missing. He and a colleague had been allowed safe passage into Fua—the same village where investigators believed Foley and Cantlie had been taken after their kidnapping—by a gang of *shabiha* gunmen before being betrayed to the Syrian authorities, bundled into a car and flown to Damascus. But even he was deeply skeptical about the *shabiha* kidnap theory. "By November, Fua was completely encircled by rebels, which is one reason why some people there wanted coverage of their situation," he told me. When he heard about Foley and Cantlie he'd approached his remaining *shabiha* contact there, a prominent gang leader, but the man knew nothing about it. "If they had been in Fua for any significant period of time this man would know. And I trust him." In any case, the general pattern was inescapable; foreign journalists arrested by the Syrian regime or its allies were almost always let go, sometimes after being paraded at a press conference in Damascus, within three to six months. Yet by the spring of 2013 nothing had been heard from either Jim Foley or John Cantlie.

Then there was the fact that the Syrian regime officials up to and including President Bashar al-Assad himself—in public interviews, in private meetings with the families and via trusted back channels and an informal canvassing of contacts within its powerful Air Force Intelligence Directorate—had always and unequivocally denied holding Foley or Cantlie. "There is no possibility that the regime has them," an intermediary involved in making one of those back-channel representations told me at the time. "Everything came back negative." In their desperation to cut through the fog of information surrounding their son's disappearance, John and Diane Foley made the journey to New York to meet Bashar Jaafari, the

Syrian government's permanent representative at the United Nations and then very much an enemy of the American government. He too denied any involvement on the part of the Syrian regime. In London, meanwhile, Cantlie's friends and family were busy badgering the British government to do more. In a letter dated shortly after Phil Balboni's speech, the Foreign Office informed Cantlie's partner that it was reaching out to the Syrian regime through consular channels but drawing a blank, and "We continue to assess it [the theory that they were being held by the regime] to be unlikely."

As the kidnappings continued, the official story of Richard Engel's abduction by *shabiha* in the area began to unravel. Rami Abdul-Rahman, director of the Syrian Observatory for Human Rights, told me that, based on his contacts on the ground and his understanding of how and by whom the kidnap video was distributed (it appeared to have been quietly uploaded by a rebel media team, early after it was made) the culprits were almost certainly a criminal gang allied to the very Islamist group that had mounted the rescue. One of the security men involved in the effort to get Engel out told me that the area in which he and his crew had been taken was a rebel enclave—and thus very unlikely to be the kind of place where pro-regime paramilitaries would hide out. Then, in a fresh article for NBC.com in April 2015, over two years after the kidnapping and prompted by an investigation by the *New York Times*, Richard Engel admitted that he'd made a mistake. The group that kidnapped his team was "a criminal gang with shifting allegiances" which "put on an elaborate ruse to convince us they were Shiite *shabiha* militiamen"; the rebels who freed them "also had ties to the kidnappers."

In the six months following the disappearance of Jim Foley and John Cantlie, however, the issue of their whereabouts was gently shelved by the rebel groups in the area. Anyone still asking questions found that the rebels didn't want to talk about it anymore. A few months after the kidnapping, a Paris staffer at Reporters Without Borders told me that activists who'd been asking about Jim Foley in rebel-held Northern Syria had been threatened. Luis Munar, a former Spanish Air Force pilot whose enthusiasm for the cause had led him to train mainstream rebels in the area, had met Foley—Foley loved to speak Spanish, and they had some friends in common—and took a personal interest in in trying to solve the case. Every time Munar asked the rebel fighters about Foley, however, they'd changed the subject. "We sleep together, we fight together. I know these people. And I had the feeling that they knew more than they were telling me." Munar concluded that the pair had been taken by rebel Islamists and were probably already dead. "James was important for [the mainstream Syrian rebels] the first month after he disappeared. Then they forgot about him."

The *shabiha* theory helped everyone forget. It let the rebels wriggle away from an issue potentially embarrassing to their own side, and passed the buck to the regime. Some reporters who'd been making discreet enquiries on the rebel side now thought better of it; maybe the investigators simply knew something they didn't. It also shifted attention away from what many Syrians already knew, that Cantlie had been kidnapped before and, as a result, a jihadi had been arrested on his return to Britain. This first kidnapping disturbed Abdulkader when he found out about it. If he'd known that one of the men had had problems with jihadis before he'd have liked to been told that in advance. He might have taken a different route. On reflection, he might not have wanted them in his car at all.

The truth was that Syria was a tinderbox of long-dormant grievances and animosities, and no more so than in the towns and villages in the north that Foley and Cantlie had made their territory. From Binnish, a city of only fifty thousand people, several thousand young men had made the journey to Iraq to fight the American army in the previous decade. Many had returned to Binnish, radicalized and ready for more; their number included a fiery orator whose nom de guerre was Abu Mohammad al-Adnani, who'd go on to become the spokesman for and one of the most powerful leaders of ISIS. It was easy for visiting journalists to miss all this—this wasn't, after all, the face that Syria's rebels wanted to present to the outside world—but both Foley and Cantlie had been having their doubts about the new Free Syrian Army. In Aleppo, Cantlie was overheard grumbling that rebel commanders were lying to him about the state of the front line. Foley, too, was beginning to wonder about the organization and enlightenment of their interlocutors on the rebel side. "As [Aleppo] continues to deteriorate," he wrote in an urgent dispatch for *GlobalPost* from the same trip to the city in October 2012, "many civilians here are losing patience with the increasingly violent and unrecognizable opposition — one that is hampered by infighting and a lack of structure, and deeply infiltrated by both foreign fighters and terrorist groups." It would be his last published story, and eerily prophetic.

So attractive had Northern Syria become as a haven for militant Islamists that by April 2013 two different outfits, Jabhat al-Nusra and the new breakaway faction calling itself Islamic State of Iraq and Sham, were squabbling over the rights to the al-Qaeda franchise. Al-Qaeda's leader Ayman al-Zawahiri had already urged his followers to kidnap Westerners to use them as leverage and soon postings on Syrian jihadi sites began to call for foreign journalists to be tried as suspected spies. Both groups, whose membership was then relatively fluid, seemed to take the hint. While filming the desecration of a Christian church that month, the Italian journalist Susan Dabbous was arrested and held with her TV crew for eleven days; hostile Islamists looked through every single image on her cameras, erasing them one by one. "I will cut your hands, so you can't write," said their emir. Dabbous told me that her kidnappers switched their allegiance from Nusra to ISIS while she was in their custody, and marked the occasion with a hearty celebration.

Given their increasing numbers of foreign fighters who didn't want their governments to know where they were, independent news gathering and the presence of international journalists was a more direct threat to the zealots of ISIS, whose power grab in Northern Syria was both swift and brutal—and accompanied by a spike in kidnappings and a campaign of intimidation. I'd seen evidence of it myself. On my return to rebel-held Aleppo City at the end of April 2013, our beaten-up car was overtaken by countless shiny people carriers, their windows tinted and with black Islamist flags hanging off the back. In a traffic jam, a North African jihadi on the back of a truck fixed me with a stare and began lowering his palm, indicating that I should put my camera down.

Journalists were being arrested for less. In May, the Danish photographer Daniel Rye Ottosen was abducted after being warned not to take photos of foreign jihadis. "We don't trust him, we need to investigate him," they told the young Syrian woman acting as his guide. When she asked if they were working for Nusra they took offense: "We are al-Qaeda," they fumed. "If you come back again, you won't leave alive." She fled to North Africa, and hasn't been back to her own country since. Three weeks after Ottosen's abduction an experienced war reporter called Didier François and his young photographer Edouard Elias were taken in the same general area, shortly after crossing the border into Aleppo Province. Just like Foley and Cantlie, they were reassured that this was only a routine investigation and they would soon be on their way. "Don't worry, we will check everything, this can be settled in one hour." Then, two weeks later, two more French journalists, Nicolas Hénin and Pierre Torres, were snatched from the street in Raqqa. Unlike Susan Dabbous, they weren't freed after a week—they were simply disappeared.

By the summer of 2013 these kidnappings looked like an organized campaign. Though almost no one would find out about their long, shared ordeal in jihadi captivity for eighteen months, two aid workers, a Brit called David Haines and an Italian, Federico Motka, had been abducted from their vehicle in March 2013 while traveling back to the Turkish border. The area they were taken from was adjacent to Bab al-Hawa, where Foley and Cantlie had been headed four months earlier. The kidnappers wore masks and looked professional; at least some spoke formal or classical Arabic, which marked them out as foreigners.

On August 3 Kayla Mueller, a political science graduate and aid worker from Arizona, was in a taxi on the outskirts of Aleppo with her Syrian boyfriend, a photographer called Omar al-Khani, when he noticed a gray people carrier on their tail. The two had met three years earlier, when Kayla had answered his advert for a flatmate and they'd struck up an immediate bond. When the revolt came to Syria, both were swept up in the exhilarating early days—Omar became a photographer-activist to document the brutalities of the Syrian regime, and Kayla fell in love.

When Omar went on the run, Kayla joined him in Turkey and helped in the effort to care for the growing number of Syrian refugees at the border. She'd volunteered for a number of different aid agencies and won plaudits for her work, but still didn't feel she was doing enough. Every time Omar slipped inside Syria Kayla would badger him to let her come too—it was important for her to see with her own eyes what was going on. Eventually, he agreed and Kayla joined him on a work trip. What followed was an exact replica of the Foley kidnapping. The people carrier overtook them and forced their taxi to a halt, after which six masked men jumped out and violently forced the pair of them into their own vehicle. It seemed obvious to Omar that they were looking for the American. "I think they were waiting for us," he told me after he was released. "This was planned."

A day later it was the turn of a stubborn, rambunctious free-lance journalist named Steven Sotloff. Sotloff, a thirty-year-old American with Israeli citizenship, was with his fixer Yosef Abobaker and three others on their way to Aleppo when they were cut off by three cars and about twenty men, almost all

of them masked. "They were waiting for us," said Yosef. "They
took him to show their power. They had information." The two
were separated almost immediately; all Yosef could hear was
Steven's voice in a nearby room, handing over his password
so they could access his computer. After fifteen days in their
grim jihadi prison, during which he could hear people being
tortured all the time, Yosef had been freed thanks to his connections with the main rebel militia in Aleppo, whom the men
from Islamic State said they were reluctant to offend. Sotloff
was still there.

The reluctance to offend went both ways. The same week,
after a year of trying, the rebels took an important regime airbase in the area, but only with the help of legions of fearless
ISIS suicide bombers; the same rebel commander who a year
earlier had told me he hadn't seen any foreign jihadis gave a
speech in which he thanked them fulsomely for their support. None of it had helped Yosef. When I phoned him the day
after his release, he sounded scared out of his wits. He couldn't
get Steven's terrified face out of his mind, and was only at his
desk to advise foreign journalists to stay away. "Don't come to
Aleppo," he kept repeating. "Do not come."

CHAPTER THREE

Proof of Life

Before the war, Abu Nabil worked in construction. He built villas in his native Aleppo, buying and selling them, and he made sure to emphasize to me, as we began talking, that he was a legitimate businessman. Since no one did business without friends in Syria's cliquey, nepotistic society, it was his good fortune to have made valuable connections in the country's labyrinthine security state. They'd come in very handy in his new venture, which was quietly procuring the release of detainees from regime prisons—and the reason he'd come to see me. A kidnapped Western journalist called Jim Foley, he happened to know, was being held incognito by the Syrian regime, and he was ready to help. "You guys want to get him out, I can get him out." How much? "A million dollars."

In the following weeks Abu Nabil, burly and ill-balanced, heaved his way into my local coffee bar in Antakya accompanied by several flunkies and expanded on his proposition in the hope that I, as another foreign journalist, might somehow be able to help. The money wasn't for him, but to grease the palms of corrupt prison officials who wanted a route out of the country. He huffed, frustrated at how long it was taking to make the deal. The plan was already in place; the only thing missing was the cash. Someone was required to stand with the money at the Jordanian border ("Lebanon is too tricky, with Hezbollah") and hand over the million only when the journalists were seen to have shown up. ("What is there to lose?") Ferrying high-profile prisoners past dozens of regime checkpoints sounded risky, but there was no need to worry—Abu Nabil could procure a letter that would smooth their path all the way to the border. He'd already met private investigators and officials from the American Embassy in Istanbul, but they'd taken his information without compensating him and his patience was wearing thin. "We have a saying: I don't want to get bitten by the same snake twice."

This was September 2013. Syria's uprising had been derailed into an ugly civil war, and only snakes like Abu Nabil and Ammar Boka'i were making any progress. Nearly a year had elapsed since Jim Foley and John Cantlie had been kidnapped and many thousands of Syrians had gone missing, too, either detained by the Syrian regime or its enemies. Taking hostages had become a weapon of war accepted on all sides, and the business of trying to get people back was now worth many hundreds of millions of dollars.

Foreign journalists—glittering luxury goods in a commodity market—were only the most visible sign of the problem. Syrians were being kidnapped for all kinds of reasons: for hard cash, to barter with other hostages, to intimidate political rivals or simply to close down independent reporting. As Syrian territory was carved up into rival fiefdoms, even the word was contentious: one person's kidnap was another's quick-thinking arrest. Like any growing industry, the brisk trade in human life had thrown up legions of useful middlemen.

Abu Nabil was one of them. He claimed that his efforts had already precipitated the release of forty-eight Syrians in transactions worth six million dollars. The money, he said, had been deposited in accounts in Iran, Egypt and Lebanon. There was corroboration too. Sometimes he'd show up with his sheepish-looking brother-in-law, but most of the time he'd arrive with rebels working with an Aleppo brigade of the Free Syrian Army. One assured me that two of his friends had got out of a Syrian prison for fifty thousand dollars; another swore that he had seen the money being handed over with his own eyes. But how could a man who spent so much time with rebels also work closely with the Syrian regime? "If we met him in Syria we would kill him. But here it's OK. He's only the middleman."

I enjoyed Abu Nabil's company. Punctuated by endless cigarettes and gallows humor, our conversations made for a lighthearted interlude amid everything else that was going on. Like many middlemen I've come across in Syria he was a gifted storyteller, and like anyone who trades in illicit information he was skilled at the tease—pretending to know more than he was letting on. "I have all the secrets," he once said, but he wasn't going to hand them over just like that. Nor was it obvious which side he was really on, and who he was working with. When I asked him about his politics he paused, as he often did, before trying to calibrate an answer that might sound professionally convincing: "The regime was deeply unjust, but the Free Syrian Army is fucked up, and the Syrian people are in the middle." But then so was Abu Nabil. His tales of why Foley had ended up where he had were rich with gripping detail—where he'd been taken, what he'd talked about during their interrogation, even the position of his cell in a prison three floors underground. John Cantlie was in an adjoining cell; his release would require a further million dollars. "They are in good hands. Not where everyone thinks, very safe," and everyone chuckled.

He was also lying—either that or his prized contacts in the Syrian regime were pulling his leg. While one or two Westerners like Austin Tice seemed to be in the hands of the regime, it was growing increasingly obvious that Foley and Cantlie, like most of the other kidnapped foreign journalists, had been taken not by the Syrian regime but by one of the many rebel groups that had grown up to fight against it. At the same time as I was hanging out with Abu Nabil, I was also getting to know a genial member of a rebel coordinating committee in Binnish. Like everyone else from the area who I spoke to, he assumed that Foley and Cantlie had been whisked away by Islamists working with Jabhat al-Nusra. Was there any chance that he'd been abducted by *shabiha*? "No." The area around Binnish and Taftanaz was full of jihadi checkpoints, one of the kidnappers was wearing a mask, there'd been no demand for money so far—all of which, he said, pointed to the involvement of Islamist militants. But since rebel battalions formed and dissolved on a monthly basis, and many of Nusra's foreign recruits had deserted it for ISIS, it wasn't clear where Foley and Cantlie had been taken since—or which middleman to approach to find out more. One afternoon I asked Abu Nabil what would happen if I ever went missing in Syria. Now that we were friends, would he make a good price for my release? Hand on heart, he promised that he would.

Just a short drive from the border, Antakya used to be part of Syria. By September 2013 it might as well have been—the Turkish city had become a huge support base for Syrian rebels and a vast diaspora of foreign jihadis who'd come from all over the world to help their cause. In this genteel antechamber to the chaos of Northern Syria, anyone who was not a spy or a soldier was a dealmaker. No one said who they were really working for, but Free Syrian Army generals, Polish intelligence agents, Saudi bag men, European hostage negotiators, American medics, Canadian security professionals and fitfully employed freelance journalists all rubbed along nicely, sometimes in the same hotel. Much of the business was done in Özsüt, the same raised-level coffee bar with an excellent view of the surrounding mountains where I had first met Abu Nabil. The whole place had become a giant bazaar dedicated to buying guns, loyalties and, occasionally, journalists.

I'd come to catch up with my old friend Yasser. I waited for a week and then, late one evening, he called and I followed him meekly to the bar of his choice. "You are not far away from a camera," he said as soon as we'd arrived, pointing at the CCTV in the corner and directing me to an empty set of tables on a lower level. When I asked about the missing journalists he rolled his eyes. "Please don't send us any more heroes," he said. "We are very disappointed with the West." Too many reporters, he maintained, had focused on hunting for stories about al-Qaeda and not enough on the iniquities of the Syrian regime. "We have a saying in Syria: if you play with fire, you get your fingers burned."

Tall and lumbering and with a spy's knack for pretending to know more than he's letting on, Yasser was a difficult person to pin down, but it quickly became apparent he was working closely with one of the investigators Kroll had assigned to the Foley case. Given the pattern of kidnappings and the presence of *shabiha* in the area, he said, he'd initially been confident that Foley had been taken to the pro-regime village of Fua and then onward to Damascus. All the local Islamist groups had denied holding him, and he'd heard that *shabiha* were arresting foreigners at checkpoints. While he was making his enquiries he'd taken a phone call from the embassy of a European country, and he'd repeated to them his belief that Foley was almost certain to be with the regime. Could this European country be one of the "very credible and confidential sources" Phil Balboni mentioned in his speech? "It's possible," Yasser said.

The truth is that Yasser's evidence for the *shabiha* theory had always been wafer-thin to non-existent. But the biggest problem with relying on him or anyone like him as a source was that, as an opposition activist, he was hopelessly, shamelessly partisan; in the same conversation he assured me that Theo Padnos, who was then conclusively known to be with Nusra, was in a regime prison. Lately, however, even Yasser's confidence in *shabiha* theory had begun to subside. Now he reckoned that it was equally possible that Foley and Cantlie had been taken by radical Islamists. If so, the most likely culprits would be one of few fringe outfits, buttressed by foreign jihadis, whose fighters were swelling the ranks of ISIS. One was a large Chechen-led brigade of foreigners known loosely as the Muhajireen. The other was the same secretive Majlis Shura al-Mujahideen that had taken John Cantlie the first time. When their leader was assassinated by mainstream rebels, the group's remaining fighters had folded themselves into the structure of larger Islamist factions. But now, freshly reconstituted under their deceased emir's brother, they were back with a vengeance, and had recently pledged allegiance to the even more extreme Islamism of ISIS. "Specialists in kidnapping," Yasser pronounced. "In most cases of foreigners, they're responsible."

Yasser and some colleagues, he said, were currently negotiating for the life of another foreign hostage held by the same group. They'd just received proof of life, and had offered seven hundred thousand dollars' ransom; if the kidnappers refused, he'd place his own bounty of two million dollars on the head of their leader. "It's like gambling," he said. "If they don't accept, I will be as good as my word."

By now it was clear that Yasser had become a minor player in Syria's burgeoning kidnap and ransom industry, bringing kidnappers and family representatives together in an effort to buy back foreign captives and—in his imagination, at least—arranging for their assassination if the deal didn't work out.

Another lead on Foley and Cantlie's whereabouts stemmed from Mahmoud, Austin Tice's Syrian friend who'd ushered him inside the country. When I dropped in on him in Antakya he looked more like a jaded, bespectacled university lecturer than the veteran fighter I'd come to expect. Twelve months earlier, however, he'd been a trusted operator, smuggling journalists and weapons into Syria and running a training camp open to all the different rebel groups. Some of his old training videos were still on his computer: one had four men wearing ski masks efficiently hijacking a jeep and emptying it of its occupants, while in the background Mahmoud barked instructions.

Mahmoud had contacts and money to spend on weapons; in rebel circles at the Turkish-Syrian border he was a good man to know. One of the first rebel leaders he was introduced to after arriving from Atlanta in the spring of 2012 was the emir of Majlis Shura al-Mujahideen. Firas al-Absi was a bulky Syrian in his forties who, after he'd studied dentistry in Aleppo and earned his jihadi stripes in Afghanistan, took temporary refuge in Saudi Arabia, Sudan and Oman before heading back toward Northern Syria, just like Mahmoud, via Turkey. Some rebels say that he met the Jordanian militant Abu Musab Zarqawi in Afghanistan; Majlis Shura al-Mujahideen was also the name for one of precursor organizations to Islamic State of Iraq, the most important predecessor of ISIS. Al-Absi was well liked among Syrian rebels like Mahmoud, even if they despised his noxious ideology. He brought battle-hardened jihadi expertise to an insurgency in which many fighters had no military experience. He was also broke, which is why he was indulging Mahmoud. When Mahmoud visited his camp in Idlib, all he saw was a row of tents and seventy men sleeping in the open air, just two kilometers away from the military airport in Taftanaz. What al-Absi lacked in manpower and resources, however, he made up for in jihadi ambition. His plan was to announce an Islamic State in Idlib; at which point, he said, he'd be pleased to offer Mahmoud the post of governor.

But, six weeks after his victory march through Bab al-Hawa, Firas al-Absi was dead in a ditch—assassinated by the Free Syrian Army who worried that the presence of his group at the Turkish border would affect their supply of weapons. While the group was then dormant after the death of its leader, its members worked closely with other rebels in the area. Not long after Foley and Cantlie went missing, Mahmoud made a call to someone who'd been on the fringes of al-Absi's group and was told: "We have them, both of them. They are alive."

Mahmoud had shared this information with anyone he thought might be interested. Another of the investigators hired by Kroll soon came calling, a man I'll call Abu Mohammed who'd also interviewed the only two eyewitnesses to the abduction. But when Mahmoud told him what he told me, Abu Mohammed wasn't impressed. "This guy was a crooked motherfucker," Mahmoud said of the Egyptian. "I met him twenty times in twenty days. He said, 'Don't tell the Foley family this, Mahmoud; they will think that their son has been killed.'" There was some talk of the Kroll investigator accompanying Mahmoud and his men to get Foley out, for which Mahmoud wanted his expenses upfront, but it hadn't gone anywhere. In any case, he'd grown to distrust the investigator and thought it better to wash his hands of the whole thing. "He was trying to tell the family that someone had kidnapped him for money and there could be a ransom," according to Mahmoud. "The last time I saw him I told him to get the fuck out."

The commercial K&R industry is built on the assumption that everything can be solved by money. The problem was that no convincing ransom demand had been forthcoming in the case of Jim Foley, nor for almost any of the others who've been kidnapped after him. "The giant question," the K&R specialist who worked on Syria cases told me, "is why they won't talk to us. My theory? It's like an internal stock market: they're trading amongst themselves instead of doing the big buyout. Instead of reaching out to families or governments, [it's] 'Maybe I should pass the potato around first…' "

Another reason to pass the potato around is that kidnapping is a labor-intensive business. A prison needs to be sourced, a regular roster of guards diverted from other duties and secure deliveries of food organized. The spike in abductions in Syria suggested a level of expertise which was being imported from Iraq. Then there were rumors that ISIS was buying up or at least soliciting foreign hostages from other rebel groups, which indicated that they must have some value to the group—and drove up prices across the board. As more foreigners went missing, the picture was of underground cells full of abused, terrified captives, held in conditions more appropriate to farm animals. Just across the border from Antakya, dotted around the verdant countryside, is an ancient cave network of Roman burial grounds and hundreds of abandoned ancient settlements known as Syria's Dead Cities. Then there was the country's belated nod to modernity—a constellation of ramshackle industrial cities that hardly anyone knew about. Far from prying eyes and often inaccessible to regime air strikes, it was in places like these that the rebels had begun to store their light weapons. They also made ideal prisons. The K&R specialist showed me the location near the border where, via a pressed panic button and GPS coordinates, he'd established that one journalist had briefly been held. "This is truly freaky," he said, before using Google Earth to pull up the image of what looked like a chicken coop.

For anyone spending more than a week in Antakya, paranoia was not unwarranted. Watching everything from a safe distance were spies from every conceivable intelligence agency, from the Syrian regime to the American State Department. One afternoon I took a discreet walk in the park with an American who was looking into a kidnapping case. The next morning a Turkish secret policeman was on the phone, demanding to know who I was. "Who's the guy with the sunhat?" he'd been asked.

The American was Barak Barfi, a think-tanker and Arab scholar whose close journalist friend Steven Sotloff had been kidnapped three weeks earlier. Clearly shaken up by the pace of events—he'd been with Sotloff the morning he went into Syria, but had pulled out of the trip at the last minute—and the fact that he was powerless to influence them, Barfi had decided to stay put in Antakya and see what could be done. Gnarly and dyspeptic, he wasn't good at making friends; unusually for Western visitors to the region, however, he spoke perfect Arabic and actually knew something about Syria. One night I visited his hotel room to find him lying on the sofa, sucking a lollipop and poring over an academic pamphlet about the plight of Syria's Alawi Muslims in the nineteenth century. On another evening I mentioned I'd secured a rare Syrian regime visa for Damascus and would be headed there in a few weeks.

Thrilled, he delivered an impromptu pep talk. "Study everything and everyone and listen carefully," he told me. "What TV channels are they watching in private? What do they really think? What are they saying to each other, behind the backs of the *mukhabarat*?" The last time he was there, he confided, he'd struck up a conversation with a kindly trader in a souk; after a cursory glance around the man had invited him into his store and firmly closed the door. What happened, I asked. Did he spill all the information? "No man, he offered to suck me off."

Despite his laid-back appearance, Barak was working around the clock. So were a few others, friends and family of the kidnapped Brits and Americans who'd made the journey to Antakya to see if they could lend a hand. They found themselves almost completely alone, turning over stones, interviewing and re-interviewing the same eyewitnesses, chasing weak leads, trying desperately to open up a line of communication with his ISIS kidnappers and get a proof of life. Or POL, as they learned to call it; acronyms unfamiliar to anyone just twelve months previously became common currency.

A bargain-basement pro bono K&R grew up around the families. Some journalists did their best to help, as did a host of unlikely volunteers from around the world. The first person to source that curious video of Austin Tice on a Syrian mountainside, for example, wasn't the FBI but an eagle-eyed thirty-something Canadian volunteer who'd found it via an obscure Syrian Twitter account one night, while she was sitting in her pajamas, stroking her cat and readying herself for bed. "The FBI didn't know anything about it when we called," she told me, "and then we worked on it all through the night." Emboldened by her success as a freelance investigator, she too had come to Antakya, and was making some progress on the Foley and Cantlie kidnapping.

Then there was John Cantlie's partner, who'd already made two trips in the spring of 2013. Smart and tenacious, she was becoming so well known in the border towns that she'd begun to be concerned for her safety. She never believed the story that Foley and Cantlie had been taken by *shabiha*, and had been working doggedly to force progress on the case. Like Yasser, her suspicion had settled on the group that took Cantlie the first time, but getting solid information six months after the event was close to impossible; the kidnappers didn't want to talk. "There's been a complete radio silence," she told me. "They don't want anything from us." Working closely with Mustafa and a local journalist, she'd heard about a Facebook page where there was rumored to be a picture of the two men in captivity. But when a friend managed to hack the page—with the help of contacts in a friendly Middle Eastern intelligence agency—there was nothing there. Then came a tip-off that the journalists had been seen standing chained to a wall in a prison near the Turkish border, their arms splayed in the style of a crucifixion; the prison was known locally as the "execution camp." One group of rebels offered to go in and rescue the journalists, but either changed their minds or came back empty-handed; they no longer had the manpower, most admitted, to take these radical Islamists on. This was to be just one of many half-baked and ultimately fruitless attempts by the families and other interested parties to get them out.

In the meantime, the numbers of the kidnapped kept piling up. By now there were four American journalists kidnapped or missing in Northern Syria. Then there were two Brits, four

French and a Dane. Add in aid workers and adventurers and
the numbers climbed higher still. Here was a close-knit community of freelance journalists and jobbing aid workers, and
their friends were going missing all around them. It was a
quiet scandal, and all the more so because of the veil of secrecy
thrown over much of the kidnapping. Jim Foley's parents
had gone public about their son's disappearance six weeks
after the kidnapping, but most of the other families, including Cantlie's, had not. There were good reasons to withhold
news of a kidnapping in the first few days, but there were also
pressing reasons why this spike in the abductions of foreigners
needed proper reporting. Since news of the kidnappings was
largely kept out of the media, few were fully aware of the risks
on the rebel side—which meant that some freelance journalists and aid workers were still going in. It also meant that no
one was able to join the dots between kidnappings. The result
was an effective conspiracy of silence between families of the
kidnapped, governments and the kidnappers themselves,
which put those Westerners who went in after them at even
greater risk.

One evening, from my Antakya hotel room, I called a Spanish photographer called Ricardo Vilanova to talk about the
risks of reporting in Northern Syria—he'd been kidnapped
before—when he surprised me with the news that he was
headed back inside. Ten days later, along with another Spanish journalist, Javier Espinosa, he was in the custody of Islamic
State. A fortnight after that came the news that another friend
of Barak Barfi, an idealistic former U.S. Army Ranger named
Peter Kassig, had been taken. On October 1, 2013, during his
third long trip inside Syria as a freelance aid worker, Kassig

was driving with five Syrian friends in an ambulance along the rocky roads in the northeast of the country when they were stopped at a checkpoint manned by half a dozen Arab Islamists. All six people in the ambulance were asked for their ID cards, and when asked what their business was in the area they told the truth: they were there to bring much-needed medical equipment and first-responder medical expertise. But what the Islamists found when they opened the back of the ambulance irked their puritanical mindset: everyone, including Peter Kassig, was smoking.

At first it would look more like an arrest than a kidnapping. The Islamists simply asked them to follow their vehicle to a local Sharia court so they could arrange the appropriate permission to deliver aid. They hadn't confiscated the aid workers' mobile phones. While they drove behind in the ambulance, Peter placed a call to an American friend, who would become his tireless advocate after the kidnapping. Kassig also had the foresight to burn some business cards with matches.

Just as in the case of Steven Sotloff, Peter was separated from the Syrians as soon as they arrived at their prison court. Kassig's colleague Muhammed remembers hearing him desperately remonstrating with his guards, arguing that "a lot of Americans are taking care of Syrian children." Soon after, they were taken to the main government building in Raqqa, which ISIS had requisitioned as its central holding prison. After three weeks and a cursory beating, Mohammed and the others were released; when he asked about Kassig the guard became cross and told him to "Forget about him." Even ISIS didn't usually stop ambulances, but Muhammed doesn't believe they were after Kassig by name. "They were looking for all foreigners. It is like a business to them." He hadn't seen Kassig in the Raqqa prison, but he knew he was there. A friend of his in a different cell was able to have a brief conversation with Kassig, both of them standing on tiptoes to talk over a partition. Another friend had noticed at least one Spanish journalist with long hair, mostly likely Ricardo Vilanova, in the same prison.

Two weeks after I left Antakya, at the end of September 2013, I made the journey via Beirut to Damascus. Everyone else was interested in the Syrian regime's use of chemical weapons, which had brought the country to the brink of war against the Western world; I was there to write about kidnapping. I arrived not long after Barack Obama had threatened the Syrian regime with a wave of air strikes, and central Damascus looked like the set for some lavish, grueling drama about the Lebanese civil war in the 1970s. Army or *shabiha* checkpoints had been thrown up on almost every corner; men with leather jackets and gray regulation Ba'athist beards hung around at road junctions, Kalashnikovs slung over their shoulders.

Flat like the bottom of a bowl under the protective gaze of Mount Qasioun, the view from the fountains of Umawiyeen Square made Damascus look as small and as intimate as a village. Most of the journalists stay here when they're in town, in a clutch of luxury hotels dotted around the square. If Austin Tice was still in the custody of the Syrian government, he wasn't far away either: within a kilometer of the square sit the crown jewels of Syria's security state as well as the headquarters of the army and air force, both of which make ideal holding centers for a high-value catch like Tice. The whole place is knotted with vast security compounds; almost all contain prisons, many deep underground. At some of the entrances are the beginnings of underground carriageways; on nearby mounds of grass men pop up from camouflaged potholes and keep walking. Since the start of the current conflict, entire streets have been cut off or sliced down the middle by colorful breezeblocks. Outside the enormous state security compound half a kilometer south, black Mercedes cars stuffed with heavies leave at great speed; pick-up trucks snake in and out of concrete chicanery, young men with heavy machine guns in the back, listing to and fro. A sentry stops a woman walking past with her child and delicately unscrews her flask, inspecting its contents for explosives.

On the drive out from Damascus to Beirut I noticed smoke billowing upward from the rebel-held suburb of Darraya to my left. It was here that Austin Tice was last seen, in the summer of 2012. The young rebel who knew Tice and who was seeking information about him in the suburbs of Damascus was no longer able to help. He'd been blown apart by the home-made mortar he was building. "Evaporated," the commander of his logistics unit told me. "There was nothing of him left." Via his friends I located a young woman who'd seen Tice taking photos in Darraya during an impromptu morale-boosting clean-up organized by rebels in the area. Through her I reached the Darrayan who knew Tice best, a twenty-nine-year-old IT graduate who'd acted as his translator.

I learned that when Tice had decided to leave Darraya, according to a rebel report prepared for his family, he'd summoned the same rebel driver who'd brought him there and the two had left together. The man was in his mid-thirties and Tice seemed to trust him: when he arrived the two hugged warmly. Much later, however, the rebels received information that the driver's son had been kidnapped by the Syrian regime, and that "the regime offered to release his son in exchange for Austin." When I phoned one of the rebels in the area from which the man had come and told him the story, he claimed to know little about it; but the driver I was talking about, he added, had since left for Saudi Arabia. The precise contours of the story were fuzzy and a little implausible, but what seemed clear was that Austin Tice hadn't been kidnapped by the regime per se—he'd been given up by a few of the rebels he trusted, either for money or to get some of their own people back.

One reason Tice might have been betrayed is because some Syrians thought he was an American soldier or spy rather than a journalist. The rebel logistics commander whose Antakya house Tice had shared before he went in told me that the deal for taking him in had always been clear: "The armed groups didn't take any money," he said, "but Austin said he was a former Marine and was going to train the fighters in exchange for access." Mahmoud was under much the same impression. But both agreed that this wasn't the behavior of a spy or undercover soldier. Tice was just another down-at-heel freelancer, talking his way into a war zone in the only way he knew how. In any case there was no evidence that he *had* helped the rebels with training or anything else. On the contrary, when it looked like they might get captured by the regime during that helicopter gunfight in Northern Syria, Mahmoud had offered Tice a hand grenade, but Tice turned it down. He was a journalist now, he'd explained, and it would compromise his position to be seen carrying a weapon.

An ambitious freelancer, Tice was encouraged by CBS News to take video while he was in Syria; along with his other possessions he left Darraya with a video camera and his MacBook. If he was delivered into the hands of the Syrian regime they would be likely to find some incriminating material on his computer—another possible reason why he hasn't been released. His military background alone would have been enough to incriminate him in the eyes of the Syrian regime, but it also might have been enough to keep him alive. Freelance journalists are a dime a dozen, but a former Marine might be someone worth keeping around. Either Tice or his computer, two sources close to the case told me, was traced to a Damascus prison facility soon after his disappearance. Whether or not he was still there, someone continued to take an interest in his case; the last Facebook message Mahmoud sent Tice on August 12, 2012 would be marked as read on October 29 the following year.

Jim Foley, on the other hand, was almost certainly not there. On the way out after a week in regime-held Syria, and after months of working to track him down, I finally caught up with the taxi-driver Abdulkader. Some people around the case thought the driver was the key to solving it; Yasser seemed convinced he was involved. But the gangly, punky, leather-clad twenty-eight-year-old who showed up five hours late on a Beirut street corner—he'd been taking paying fares around North Lebanon—didn't look like he could be involved in a kidnapping gang. "Everybody who asks about this case only wants money," he said. "That's why I wanted to help you." The only thing he remembered about the kidnappers was that at least one looked a little darker than a Syrian and was likely a Bedouin or a Gulf Arab. His accent when he barked *"Igaad"* ("Sit down") at the journalists was that of a Bedouin or a Gulf Arab; it was not at all the way *shabiha* from Fua would pronounce it. And there was something else: one of them had long, flowing hair, much more stylish and modern than the jihadis Abdulkader had seen around the area before. Before they'd driven off they'd taken Abdulkader aside and asked him: "Have these men paid you? Did you get your money?" It was exactly the kind of thing righteous Islamists say to butter up the locals when they arrive in an area—unlike everyone else, we are not going to steal your stuff—and certainly not how a *shabiha* from Fua would address a rebel from Binnish. Unless this was a cunning false-flag operation, mounted on the hoof by beleaguered security forces in a ferociously hostile area, the kidnappers were rebels and not with the Syrian regime.

In Antakya, Mustafa told much the same story. He also confided that he recognized one of the kidnappers. "I saw him before," he said, among the ranks of foreign jihadis around his local area. The very fact Mustafa recognized him made it extremely unlikely he was a *shabiha* from Fua. In any case, given the rebel sympathies of Mustafa and his work with foreign journalists, regime paramilitaries would hardly have let him escape with his life. Mustafa had been discreetly making his own enquiries ever since the kidnapping, and had recently been informed by a senior Jabhat al-Nusra commander that that the journalists were still alive and with the new Islamic State of Iraq and Sham group in Aleppo, but "we can't do anything because we are not on good terms with them." It sounded like interesting information, but it might have been another tall story or elaborate play for money—and there was no way to prove it. When Mustafa asked what ISIS could want, holding them for so long and in such incredible secrecy, the man from Nusra had shrugged. "They're a big deal," he said. The implication was that Foley and the other kidnapped journalists might be useful as an unspecified trump card. I kept coming back to something Yasser had told me, over our late drink in that Antakya bar. "They might keep Americans for special occasions," he'd said, as if they were bottles of good wine. He'd meant it about the Syrian regime and not about the Islamists, about Austin Tice and not Jim Foley, but it seemed increasingly appropriate all round.

If the Islamic State of Iraq and Sham was behind the kidnapping of Jim Foley, John Cantlie and the others, Antakya's cottage industry of ransom negotiators and hopeful middlemen was largely a waste of everyone's time. This glut of orchestrated, open-ended, industrial-scale kidnapping of foreign hostages looked more like the Iran hostage crisis, or something from 1980s Beirut.

The night before I left Damascus I received an email from the same genial rebel activist who traveled back and forth to Binnish and Antakya and who'd been helping me with my enquiries. He had urgent news, he wrote. It wasn't Islamic extremists who'd taken Foley and Cantlie after all. The real culprits, he'd discovered, were a shadowy criminal gang, and now they were ready to negotiate and produce a proof of life. They wanted payment even for this information, and for someone to bring more money to a remote location in Northern Syria to find out more. I didn't believe him, so I didn't go.

CHAPTER FOUR

The European Connection

When the call came on November 9, 2013, Michael Foley was on the way to a wedding. On the other end of the phone was an excitable Belgian, talking fast. "I'd received dozens of calls offering information," said Michael, "so I initially I blew it off. But because I was in the car I listened to what he had to say." What Dimitri Bontinck told him was that his eighteen-year-old son Jejoen had recently been released by Syrian jihadis. While in captivity, Jejoen Bontinck had befriended Michael's older brother Jim. Their conversations continued throughout the day and into the evening; at one point Dimitri relayed information directly from Jejoen, who was now incarcerated in an Antwerp prison on terrorism charges. "It was just the amount of information behind the story, the description of the family. And he didn't say he had current access to Jim, which is what most of the people who were lying said. Like, 'Hey, if you give me ten thousand dollars for travel expenses I can get to him.'

This was different. Dimitri was saying, 'My son was with him a few months ago.' " The message was simple: Jejoen had promised Foley and Cantlie that, if he ever made it out, he'd let their families know they were alive. Now he was out.

The call from Dimitri Bontinck changed everything. "I was so excited," says Foley's mother Diane. "It confirmed that Jim was alive; we had not heard a single thing." It had been almost a year since the two journalists had gone missing; all of the Foleys' attempts to find their son had been dashed, but it hadn't stopped them trying. While Diane Foley sent furious emails to the U.S. State Department and the FBI, and knocked on the door of foreign embassies—she'd quit her job in the spring, which gave her more time to spend on the search—it had been Michael Foley's responsibility to keep an eye on the campaign website and the information that it was bringing in. Anything promising would immediately be forwarded to the investigators and Jim Foley's editor at *GlobalPost*, Phil Balboni, but mostly it was garbage, just naked plays for money. "So many false leads, promises of information," says Foley's father John. "We'd actually been scammed by a friend of Jim's. A guy who he'd stayed with in Syria, eaten with." The call from Dimitri Bontinck had also followed an approach through the website, but in this case Michael Foley was sufficiently intrigued to share it with his mother. "I'll talk to him," she said. "It doesn't hurt to talk to him."

When Diane Foley spoke directly to Jejoen Bontinck, she knew it was genuine. The previous February, he told her, he'd followed a group of young Belgian Islamists to Syria to fight against the regime. But he hadn't realized what he'd signed up for, and quickly fell out with his comrades. He'd spend most of his eight months in Syria in the jihadis' prisons, and it was during one of those periods of incarceration, in an Islamist compound in Aleppo City, that he'd shared a cell with Jim Foley and John Cantlie for three weeks. He and Foley even seemed to have formed a bond: as a former teacher in America's inner cities, Jim knew how to mentor troubled young people. Meanwhile Dimitri Bontinck had traveled to Aleppo and raised media hell looking for his son; eventually the emir of the group holding Jejoen had tired of the crazy Belgian father and let Jejoen make his way home. Now the former jihadi was happy to help in whatever way he could. "He gave us all this detail," said Diane Foley. "The prison in Aleppo, the room, the entrance, how you get in and out."

The Foley security team moved fast. While the FBI and Scotland Yard would dispatch their own detectives to Belgium in due course, one of *GlobalPost*'s investigators was in Antwerp within the week and talked his way into the prison. Each prison visit was to last only an hour, and visits were strictly rationed. Pen and paper weren't allowed, but there was so much to say and remember—prison locations, the names of guards and prisoners—that the investigator wrote everything down in secret. While middlemen like Abu Nabil had dug up obscure information about Foley's background from the internet, Bontinck knew intimate details about Foley's family, home and work history that he couldn't have read online. He was able to report that Cantlie had tattoos on both arms, one of prison bars with two hands behind them, the other the Superman logo. He was even able to tell them what car Cantlie's partner drove, and the nationality of her gym instructor. Foley had given Bontinck the phone number of his mother and an email address for his brother Michael. Cantlie had handed over the number for his partner's landline and her email address, and, presumably as a way to prove his bona fides, his own private email address too. For the first time, here was real proof of life.

The task now was to bring them home. The rebel compound Jejoen Bontinck identified was well known locally and was equally well fortified. I'd passed it myself in the spring. Inside was a children's hospital, the offices of a telephone company and an eye hospital, all of which had been divvied up by the various rebel groups and all of which seemed to contain prisons; it was in basement of the latter that Jejoen encountered Cantlie and Foley. All the activity took place upstairs—the eye hospital had been turned into a working Sharia court—but downstairs, in a semi-underground area, was a secret prison with about ten large cells. Their cell measured about four meters by eight, with beige walls and a cold stone floor. There were mattresses and books, and in the wall was a window that could be opened easily. They'd only been in the building since the end of July—a month before Bontinck met them—and they'd been joined by a naïve German called Toni Neukirch who'd come to Syria to help the rebel cause.

Foley, Cantlie, and Neukirch were being treated conspicuously better than anyone else in the prison, because all were now Muslim. Foley and Cantlie told Bontinck that they'd converted many months earlier; the guards were skeptical at first, but eventually came to believe them. They'd even taken Arabic *kunyas* or *noms de guerre*; Foley's was Abu Hamza, while Cantlie's was Abu Zaid.

The French hostage Didier François first saw Foley and Cantlie in the eye hospital's basement on July 28. The meeting didn't last long, but he learned of their conversion: "He and John were moved to another cell twenty minutes after we arrived. The excuse given to us by a guard was they were Muslims, so they could not stay with us." Jejoen Bontinck believed their conversion too. "I can't open their hearts," he told me, "but they asked me a lot of detailed questions regarding Islam. According to that I can still say it's sincere." The three of them talked a great deal about faith and Islam—about how their lives weren't good before, about how Foley should get married, about how Cantlie should behave around his partner until she converted. Very likely they were telling Bontinck what they thought he wanted to hear. Here was a teenage jihadi they'd only just met and who, unlike them, was only under house arrest: he appears to have been sent to the cell first to bring food, and to perform *da'wah* (religious outreach) by helping them on their journey to Islam.

In any case, the men's conversion seemed to help. Apart from Neukirch, Foley and Cantlie were the only prisoners allowed to use the basement toilet without a blindfold. "They were treating them perfectly in that prison," says Bontinck. "If they were sick the doctor would come. The door was always open. People in charge would bring cookies and drinks from the market, and sit and talk with them. Show them videos, bring books. They didn't do that with other prisoners." Having been very skinny when they arrived, both men were soon in relatively good shape. Cantlie had even improvised a fitness regime, using buckets of water as makeshift weights. While it's unlikely they completely trusted him, the pair clearly grew fond of Bontinck. When they weren't discussing religion, they told him stories from their reporting adventures: Foley recounted the terrible experience of a colleague being killed beside him in Libya. They also talked about movies—Bontinck had been to Washington and Miami as a youth and adored American cinema—and John impressed the youngster with his previous career as a games tester for Sega. He even taught Jejoen how to build a computer. To pass the time, the three played guessing games like Twenty Questions. Foley and Cantlie made plans to holiday in Belgium after they were released, and Cantlie invited Bontinck to visit him at his London home. From time to time the man in charge, a tall, lanky Dutch-Moroccan with a liking for sunglasses known as Abu Obeida al-Maghrebi, swung by to say hello.

It was relatively nice while it lasted. By the time Bontinck left, he said, the general feeling was that the journalists had been punished enough—there they might be eligible for release, or at least given the choice to swap prison for a jihadi training camp. Cantlie, desperate for any movement, seemed keen. Bontinck had mooted another idea, that Cantlie might benefit from the same kind of house arrest that he was under—a kind of jihadi probation in which perhaps he could bring his partner to join him in Syria and then make his way back after a few years.

It is not clear whether Cantlie really believed any of it. He told Bontinck that a Dane and Italian were being held in the same basement, and that he reckoned their hosts were planning to release them, but only for a huge ransom. Bontinck once asked Cantlie what he was going to do if he was released, and he'd replied: "I don't know if I will ever be allowed to go home." When the time came for Bontinck to gather his stuff,

Cantlie became very emotional—both he and Foley were happy that Bontinck was going home, but disappointed they weren't going too. "I have been here before," he said. It was true in more ways than one; most of his jailers came from the same Majlis Shura al-Mujahideen group, brimming with Europeans, which held him hostage the first time.

Most accounts of the rise of Islamic State in Syria see it as an offshoot of Jabhat al-Nusra, the Syrian-led militia that was lent weaponry and expertise by the Islamic State of Iraq in the early months of the armed rebellion before it swore allegiance to al-Qaeda.

But the idea that ISIS was a blow-in from Iraq was only one side of the story, and the least interesting. As early as the summer of 2012, nearly a year before the birth of the Islamic State of Iraq and Sham, Majlis Shura al-Mujahideen was independently floating the idea of an Islamic State in Syria. After the assassination of Firas al-Absi in the summer of 2012 its fighters scattered and took cover in other Islamist factions in the area. It wasn't long, however, before the emir's younger brother Amr began rebuilding the group. Amr al-Absi was a brooding, charismatic man with penetrating eyes and a skeletal physique; he'd acquired the latter during his years in Sednaya, the infamous prison in which the Syrian regime likes to house its Islamist prisoners. Soon after he was released he acquired the *kunya* Abu Athir. By the time he moved his operational base to Aleppo, the revived Majlis Shura al-Mujahideen had swollen to several thousand armed men. With no sign of the heavy weapons promised by their international supporters, other rebel groups fell back on their support.

They were strong fighters. Along with another militia whose fighters hovered around the Turkish border, Katiba al-Muhajireen (the brigade of emigrants), then led by a red-bearded Georgian calling himself Omar al-Shishani, Majlis Shura al-Mujahideen was soon ferrying scores of European jihadis into Northern Syria via the porous Turkish border and the official crossings that had fallen into rebel hands. Relations between the two groups were excellent—but whereas Eastern Europeans flocked to al-Shishani, al-Absi drew in and trained up hundreds of young Belgian, Dutch, French and German men. A Dutch fighter who'd been with Majlis Shura al-Mujahideen during this period told me, when I phoned him in Aleppo, that this influx of Western Europeans was largely due to Abu Athir. "He was very important in the development of the Islamic State. He saw that a lot of brothers were coming from Europe and that he could use them, mix them with the locals. And those who came were eager, because he was treating them well." In the spring of 2013 Abu Athir was also one of the first to join his fighters with the brand-new Islamic State of Iraq and Sham; in return, they made him their governor of Aleppo. By the time it was rolled out, ISIS wasn't so much a diktat from Iraq as a meeting of jihadi minds—one buttressed by networks of recruits that had already been established in Europe.

Jejoen Bontinck was one of those recruits. One afternoon after his return I sat outside a chic, minimalist coffee bar in the center of Antwerp waiting for him to join me for a late lunch. We were in touch via an online instant-messaging service, and

Bontinck kept sending me messages to ask me where I was and apologize for the delay. Eventually he messaged me that he was in the vicinity.

"Are you outside?" he wrote.

Looking around, I replied that I was.

"I'm behind the corner."

Before he'd even be seen, Bontinck was casing both me and the joint. He had every reason to be nervous; thanks to him, some of his former jihadi friends were headed for prison. A month after we met, in one of the highest profile Belgian court cases for years, he and forty-five other members of an Islamist cell called Sharia4Belgium would go on trial in Antwerp, along with the organization itself, which was accused of luring young Belgians away from mosques, training them in preaching and combat and readying many for jihad. Most were being tried *in absentia*, since they were still in Syria. Some were already dead, but since there was no official proof of their deaths their names were added to the charge sheet anyway. Almost all would end up with jail terms. As the star witness for the prosecution, Bontinck would escape with a suspended sentence.

It would be a lot to handle for any teenager, but especially one who'd been through what Bontinck had. We met exactly two weeks after Jim Foley had been killed, and he was clearly still upset. He blamed both sides. If the Americans hadn't mounted air strikes of Islamic State's positions in Iraq, he said, maybe Foley would still be alive. Dreadlocked and streetwise, Bontinck looks like a pop-star heartthrob; as a youth he was an accomplished break-dancer, even appearing on a Belgian TV show impersonating Michael Jackson. At age fifteen, he fell in love with a Muslim girl and became a student of Islam. It was through her that he came across the young men from Sharia4Belgium and their leader, a street preacher called Fouad Belkacem.

Jejoen's parents were divorced, and he'd been bullied at school. Sharia4Belgium seems to have given him and other impressionable young men purpose and puritanical rigor—"a good feeding up," as the former Dutch Majlis Shura al-Mujahideen fighter put it when I called him in Aleppo. Maybe Bontinck needed it, and maybe it hadn't entirely worn off. It was clear during our meeting that he maintained a grudging respect for some of the fighters he'd met in Syria; Abu Athir was "a good man and a bad man. He is a very special guy, very apart." For a time Bontinck even had his own *kunya*. Did he fight in Syria? "No I didn't," he said, and it was clear that part of him missed the adventure and the short-lived camaraderie. His motto on the instant-messaging service we both used was "So try to emulate them if you aren't like them, for emulating the noble is success."

His love of dancing and other earthly pleasures made Bontinck a wayward recruit, but he'd answered the call to go to Syria in February 2013. After being smuggled across the border from Turkey he was picked up by friends from Sharia4Belgium and driven straight to a huge villa in the northern Aleppo village of Kafr Hamra, which Abu Athir had sequestered for Majlis Shura al-Mujahideen. The villa was equipped with several flat screen TVs, a PlayStation and a swimming pool. Around two hundred fighters from the group lived in it and in other palatial quarters in the same area, and there were more Europeans than locals among them.

Bontinck's account of his time at a nearby jihadi training camp is revealing. There were three different camps: one for Jabhat al-Nusra, another for Omar Shishani's Eastern Europeans and a third for Abu Athir's group. Even when he was imprisoned and being brutalized, the experience was oddly intimate, like being in a second home. At one point in his torture, during which Bontinck was beaten with electrical cables and suffered a mock execution at the hands of Abu Athir, the Dutch prison chief took the trouble to inquire after the good health of Sharia4Belgium's leader Fouad Belkacem—and to wonder whether Bontinck had gone to one of Belkacem's demos in the run-down Brussels municipality of Molenbeek.

Bontinck's father would also face a mock execution supervised by Abu Athir, and at around the same time. When he realized where Jejoen was, Dimitri Bontinck made the journey to Syria to try to track him down. It was an extraordinarily brave thing to do, to dive into war-torn Aleppo Province, but the uncomfortable truth was that he was in fact the source of many of his son's troubles. Jejoen was being tortured because his fellow jihadis were convinced he was an Israeli spy—an opinion they'd formed after discovering a text from Dimitri promising to use his mythical friends in Mossad to get his son out. When I met Dimitri Bontinck for afternoon "aperitifs" in Antwerp he begrudgingly admitted his mistake. "Mossad are the best intelligence service in the world," he shrugged. "And who would have thought that others would be reading the message?"

Pink-faced and permanently furious, Dimitri Bontinck made engaging company, but he was also a motor-mouth and a braggart. Since he'd accompanied his son back from Syria he'd forged a new career as a "jihadi hunter," allegedly venturing deep into ISIS-controlled territory to bring back other young Belgian jihadis. Some of the details of his trips inside Syria were open to question; journalists wrote them down anyway. One story that did ring true, however, was his account of a visit he paid to Abu Athir's villa in April 2013. Judging by the numbers of shoes in the hall, Dimitri reckoned that there were about a hundred young men living in the villa, and judging by the accents most of them seemed to be European. The living room was full of guns, grenades and suicide belts; everyone inside was wearing a mask and Abu Athir, then recovering from a war wound, lay in the middle.

When he arrived, Dimitri Bontinck patiently explained that he was looking for Jejoen, but Abu Athir denied any knowledge of the name. The conversation was pleasant enough, but when it concluded and Bontinck rose and shook his hand the Syrian refused to let go. Then they pounced from behind. Several jihadis held Bontinck's hands behind his back and blindfolded him; others threw him on the floor and ripped off his clothes, then and dragged him to a room upstairs; at one point, according to Bontinck, about nine or ten masked men were beating him with their fists and feet. "They were shaking and turning everything inside and out to see if there was a hidden transmitter: they even took the SIM card out of my mobile phone. They are professionals, they are good." Some spoke English and French; when they told him they were going to translate the texts on his phone, he knew there must be Dutch jihadis in the group as well.

Bontinck kept protesting that he was simply a father looking for his son, but it had little effect. Every answer he gave was

ferried downstairs to Abu Athir, who sent back supplementary
questions. Eventually Dimitri persuaded the jihadis he was
telling the truth, but it was a close thing. At one point he felt a
gun being placed in his mouth and heard the sound of it being
cocked. "You are CIA. Who told you your son is here? Who
told you the Belgians are here?"

The men interrogating Dimitri Bontinck were right to be
concerned about spies. Sharia4Belgium had been under constant surveillance and harassment by the Belgian authorities
since it was established in 2010. Shortly after Fouad Belkacem
was arrested in June 2012 it disbanded. At that point many
of its devotees seemed to have decided to try their luck in
Syria. Almost all hooked up with Abu Athir's Majlis Shura al-
Mujahideen. For Jejoen Bontinck's lawyer Kris Luyckx, the
relationship between the two was an open-and-shut case. "It's
clear that all those people who were with Sharia4Belgium
went over there," he told me when I visited him in Antwerp.
"I am not saying that they had a real organization, airplanes
et cetera. It was very subtle, of course. They look for people,
influence them to do that. It is a very thin line." The Antwerp
trial documents run to some fourteen thousand pages, and
tell a powerful story about the relationship between the ennui
felt in some European inner cities and the rise of Islamic State.
In photos obtained by the Belgian police, street-smart young
men are pictured doing *da'wah* on behalf of Sharia4Belgium
on the streets of Antwerp, handing out leaflets to passersby,
diligently proselytizing their new religion.

The Belgian prosecutors argued that Sharia4Belgium was
working closely with the British Islamist Anjem Choudary,
whose Sharia4UK pre-dated its Belgian equivalent and seemed

to have been the parent organization. Some of the internal documents used by the Belgian group were titled in English; one was "The Virtues of Killing a Non-believer for the Sake of Allah," while another concerned itself with the "virtue of an individual or small group immersing themselves within a large army of non-believers in search of martyrdom and causing damage to the enemy." Choudary and his lieutenants, claimed the prosecutors, often traveled to meet their Belgian counterparts, and Choudary was clearly a leading source of guidance to Sharia4Belgium.

One intercepted telephone call between Belkacem and Choudary, on May 31, 2012, has the latter counseling the Belgian on how to deal with one of the "brothers" who, like Jejoen Bontinck, had strayed from the flock. "They need to be cultured, they need to be told. They need to be informed," he says. Choudary, the student of Belgian jihadism Pieter van Ostaeyen told me, was "the guru, mentor, the inspiration" for Belkacem, who, with a string of convictions for petty crime, was considered something of a "nitwit" by local imams. Jejoen Bontinck told me that he himself met Choudary on several occasions, when he came to Belgium to teach, but believes that he had nothing to do with the trafficking of jihadis to Syria. "He is a great guy, a very smart guy. He came to Belgium a lot of times and gave us lessons, but I don't think there is a link. I'm sure of it, otherwise he would be in prison."

He may well be right. Many young men in Western countries are drawn to Syria not because of fiery preachers like Choudary but because of things they read on the darker corners of the web. But the irony of our attempts to understand the motives and the mysterious barbarism of Islamic State is that we could do worse than look to the rumbling discontent in our own backyard. Before they were emblazoned on huge posters in Syria, Islamic State slogans like "Submission to Allah," "Democracy will bring oppression," and "Sharia will bring justice" were being carried on demos by tiny Choudary-linked groups such as Muslims Against Crusades, Sharia4UK and Islam4UK.

From Bosnia to Chechnya, the lure of jihadi migration (*hijrah*) among young men is nothing new, but the numbers traveling to Syria were unprecedented. By 2015 analysts estimated that there were around twenty thousand foreign jihadis in the country. The majority were from surrounding Arab countries, but at least five thousand were thought to be European. If a few seemed perfectly suited to being prison guards for Western hostages, maybe it's because they already knew the drill. When he taught Arabic in a prison near Antwerp, Pieter van Ostaeyen saw petty criminals morph over the space of a few months into zealous Islamists under the influence of powerful fundamentalist Salafi preachers. The way he sees it, puritanical Islamism has become just another prison gang culture, much like Aryan Nation in the United States. "Inside the prison there was a variety of sub-cultures; there was the druggy sub-culture, and then you had the Islamist sub-culture. Each had their ringleader. Some guys adhered to both."

Along with London, Antwerp has become one of the key European hubs for jihadi recruitment to Syria. Many of Jejoen Bontinck's former Sharia4Belgium associates hail from the same district of the city, Borgerhout, where he still hangs out. Some of them have also done time in prison. It's the reason Bontinck is now nervous about meeting strangers. Kris Luyckx told me that he had, as a young lawyer doing pro bono work, represented a few defendants in the Sharia4Belgium trial when they were juveniles: the charges were drugs, petty theft or assault. "I know three of them," he told me. "Two are dead in Syria."

It would be easy to conclude that the young men's interest in hardline religion was bound up with their slide into criminality, but in many cases it seems to be the opposite—some of these young men seem to have sought out jihad as a kind of redemption, an act of atonement for their misdeeds. "Jejoen was looking for an identity and a group where he would be accepted," was the only way his lawyer could explain it. "If you want to make up with Sharia4Belgium [a friend told him], go to Syria and everything will be forgotten. That was a very big reason why he left Belgium."

It might also have been the reason he wanted to go back. In January 2014, four months after we met, and shortly before he was to be sentenced, Jejoen Bontinck was arrested at Brussels airport while trying to board a flight to Turkey. The most likely explanation is he wanted to rejoin and redeem himself in the eyes of his jihadi friends in Syria.

"How did you come here? Why are you here?" were among Jejoen Bontinck's first questions to Jim Foley and John Cantlie in the eye hospital's basement prison. Over the next three weeks they answered as best they could. They began with their kidnapping, nine months previously; among the jihadis who'd cut off their taxi that day was at least one they'd seen before.

They recognized him from the internet café; it must have been the one who was wearing a beret and who baulked at Cantlie's attempts at conversation. The kidnappers had all been wearing masks, but before they'd been blindfolded they'd noticed—according to Jejoen—that he was wearing the same clothes.

The first six months of their captivity had been a descent into purgatory, almost all of it at the hands of the British guards who took over their custody. Their first prison was a garage with a skylight. They had only dirty water to drink and very little food, and from the beginning the behavior of their guards was cruel in the extreme. Their guards were masked at all times, and Foley and Cantlie's best guess, based on their accents, was that most were from east London and of Pakistani or Bangladeshi descent. For the most part, their guards' Arabic was conversational and not fluent. Later they'd have trouble translating into English the statements that the hostages were being asked to read. One, a well-built man in his mid-twenties, said he was a former boxer. Another one said that he was a doctor. But they were liars, Foley and Cantlie concluded—one lied so often they called him Pinocchio. Just like the last time John had been held hostage, making up nicknames for his oppressors was a way to lighten the mood, and to cauterize the fear.

The guards had been Brits then too, so he knew what kind of brutality to expect this time. On one occasion he was forced to stand chained for three days until he was delirious. The chains left scars on his feet. Foley had it worse, simply because he was American. Based on an alleged photo of him in U.S. army uniform (according to Foley's parents, it was actually a picture of his brother Mark), the guards were convinced he was a CIA agent. The guard who claimed to be a boxer appears to have used Foley as a punchbag. Foley showed Bontinck the marks on his arm from having been beaten several times in the same place by the boxer's fists. Foley had also been shackled and beaten with cables, probably while being hung upside down. "You could see the scars on his ankles," Jejoen told me.

Here were inner-city British men setting about other Westerners, and doing so largely because of a frustrated animus with their lives back home—a home likely just a few miles away from John Cantlie's in London. Much of the torture was, the guards claimed, "punishment" for real or alleged infractions; one involved shooting Tasers at the prisoners' hands and bodies. The worst followed two attempts to escape. The first time, Foley and Cantlie later told the Spanish journalist Javier Espinosa, they'd tried picking the locks of their handcuffs using a makeshift skeleton key but were immediately caught. "They didn't get anywhere," another of the freed hostages told me. "They were very unlucky, and were caught." On the second attempt Foley made it out of the cell but Cantlie didn't; not wanting to leave his friend behind, Foley gave himself up. Each failed attempt brought terrible consequences.

At some point in early spring 2013, Foley and Cantlie were joined by two aid workers, the Briton David Haines and the Italian Federico Motka. The "punishments" continued; at times, the four hostages were forced to box one another—the prisoners grimly called it the Royal Rumble. It was a terrible thing, to be made to fight each other on pain of torture, but the four men went through the motions. "The forced fighting was sometimes John and James together, sometimes it was John and James against two others," says Bontinck. "The losers would be tortured. It happened a couple of times." Another freed European hostage described it as "Everyone boxing against each other, two against two and one against one. They were all terrible. They were so weak, basically useless. John won."

Foley and Cantlie had been moved five times in the first six months of their captivity. They couldn't tell Bontinck where they'd been; probably because they had no idea, and nor would many of the ordinary grunts protecting them. From the first moment of their captivity, all their non-Syrian guards wore masks. When they were moved, which was regularly, they might have been made to wear masks too. It explained why they'd been made to disappear so efficiently—these people were professionals, working in a small, very disciplined team and refining their trade. The best they could say was that the kidnap was the "initiative of a local brigade" of Jabhat al-Nusra that hadn't been officially sanctioned by the organization. But kidnappers in Syria aren't known for their transparency, and they might not have been telling Jejoen the whole truth. One likely culprit was Majlia Shura al-Mujahideen, which had taken John Cantlie the first time and one of whose number, the doctor Shajul Islam, was charged with Cantlie's kidnapping on his return to the UK. According to one of the freed European hostages, Cantlie was however sure that there were different kidnappers the second time around: "The persons who took him the first time are not the same persons—John told me this—but potentially people close to them. They searched his computer and found his debrief for Scotland Yard and an interview he gave in which he said his kidnappers were amateurs. And he was badly treated for that. And then they found out about the doctor, and there was"—there was a long pause—"retaliation."

If Shajul Islam's impending court case didn't precipitate the kidnapping, it certainly didn't help Cantlie's hope of an early release, even though Cantlie seems to have believed the doctor was personally innocent. "They found out [who he was]," another freed European told me, "and they were really happy to have him. But I'm not sure that's why they were taken. They will never say. They were giving Cantlie some information on the fact that the trial was a factor and that they would keep him because of this—so he could not give his testimony and there was a guy who would be released." The charges against Shajul Islam were duly dropped in November 2013. A week later I met with his lawyers to share my suspicions about Majlis Shura al-Mujahideen and to request Islam's help in understanding the group. It would be the first of three meetings, and my messages were duly passed on, but he didn't want to meet another journalist, and he didn't want to help.

One thing Foley and Cantlie did seem to be clear about was that the British guard who killed Jim Foley on that gory video had been there from the moment they were taken. When some of the freed European hostages watched the execution videos, they recognized him by his holster. "He was kidnapped by the one who killed him," one told me. "I am sure of that." Independently, another hostage told me the same thing. The fact that the same Brit could have been involved in their incarceration over nearly two years was another reason to think that this wasn't the work of al-Qaeda's Syrian wing but something new and much stranger—and better organized than anyone had imagined. Their initial kidnappers, according to a European former hostage who had spent much more time with Foley and Cantlie than Bontinck, "were ISIS from the beginning." In a face-to-face interview in Europe I asked another freed hostage who was responsible for the early British-managed period of imprisonment and he was unambiguous: "This was ISIS before ISIS."

The growing booty of high-value foreign hostages might even have helped broker the deal that led to the group's birth. By the time Jejoen Bontinck arrived in Syria most arriving British jihadis were attaching themselves to the loose, largely Chechen-led bands of foreign fighters which roved around the same areas of Northern Syria known as the *muhajireen*. Sometime in the late spring or early summer, according to Bontinck, the British guards who held Foley and Cantlie handed them to Abu Athir: exactly the moment at which his outfit and elements of these *muhajireen* joined forces to help build the brand-new Islamic State of Iraq and Sham. His best guess is that the transfer "was about power." The most likely explanation is that Foley and Cantlie were abducted by one tightly knit band of *muhajireen* and were then passed to Abu Athir when both groups pledged allegiance to the new organization. Their handover to the arbitration of the "courts" may well have been part of the dowry, or at least a gesture of good faith, between two groups who'd just thrown in their lot with the Islamic State.

The British guards were so effortlessly sadistic that John Cantlie told Jejoen he'd prayed to go to a better place. The problem, according to another freed hostage, was that the British never believed in their conversion to Islam. "We are now getting rid of you," were their parting words, before they handed Jim and John over. "Enjoy the rest of your time with us."

From the Brits Foley and Cantlie were taken to a safe house where they were fed and treated well, and not tortured any more. Then they were sent to the eye hospital in the Aleppo compound, which was under the control of Abu Athir and his Dutch head of security Abu Obeida al-Maghrebi. Abu Obeida *was* convinced by their conversion—he talked to them, arranged better food for them and gave them special privileges as Muslims.

Others had fared less well. Immediately after their abduction, Kayla Mueller and Omar al-Khani were driven to the same compound and deposited in different cells. Shortly after her abduction, according to a girl I spoke to who met her later in her captivity, Kayla Mueller had some of her fingernails pulled out under interrogation—accused of smuggling, of being a journalist, and of being American. For the first two weeks al-Khani was tortured every day, too, mostly at the hands of Arab guards. "They were saying—you are CIA, and bringing *kufr* [unbelievers] to the Islamic State." In the same basement, the journalist Nicolas Hénin was repeatedly being punched in the face by a fellow Frenchman called Mehdi Nemmouche, who was convinced he was a spy, during interrogations sometimes supervised by al-Maghrebi. After returning to Europe, in May 2014, Nemmouche would be charged with the murder of four people in a crazed attack on the Jewish Museum in Brussels.

Even the respite enjoyed by Foley and Cantlie was to prove short-lived. From Aleppo, Foley and Cantlie would be sent to another prison run by a Frenchman, and after that they'd be reunited with their worst tormentors—the British jihadis. At each stage in their frightening passage through Islamic State's network of prisons, the only certainty is that their mid-level guards were always European. There was a certain symmetry, which suggested that Islamic State's campaign of kidnapping foreign hostages and its reliance on foreign recruits were joined at the hip. To European jihadis, nosey journalists or aid workers from their home countries asking questions or taking pictures was an immediate risk to their security, but at the same time they could be used as a weapon against the governments the jihadis detested. In due course, Islamic State would write emails demanding ransom money from European governments, families and charities for some of the hostages' return.

Until Jejoen Bontinck made it back to Europe, no one would know the full horror of what was going on. Security was tight: even some of those held in the eye hospital would have no idea who was being held in the other cells. Omar al-Khani had no idea Foley and Cantlie were being held in in the same basement prison as him, but he did know they were other Westerners. One of his cellmates told him there were two Frenchmen in another cell, and he could hear what he thought might be people speaking French but, held behind the hospital's concrete walls and impregnable steel doors, he did not actually see anyone. Bontinck's return to Belgium blew all that secrecy apart. With the prison layout and other detail his son brought back, Dimitri Bontinck remains convinced that a rescue could have been mounted; that Foley and Cantlie, at the very least, could have been brought home. "They were getting better food than the other prisoners. This was the way to get them out; the food was always delivered from outside, by the same guy at the same times, three times a day. This was October 2013. They could have organized a mission, and they could have been free."

It was typical Dimitri, and wide of the mark. Beginning at the end of August and presumably for reasons of security, the foreign hostages were spirited out of Aleppo City to a place called Sheikh Najjar in the industrial suburbs. By the time they left the compound, the foreigners were all being held in two cells; François and seven others were in one and Foley, Cantlie and Toni Neukirch were in the other. That made a total of eleven; twelve including Kayla Mueller, who was being held in a third, separate room. Their numbers were being added to all the time, and the fact that they were being herded together must have been unnerving for everyone. It meant that the ad hoc abduction of troublesome Westerners was giving way to a much bigger plan.

CHAPTER FIVE

Kidnapping Inc.

In peacetime, the journey to Sheikh Najjar at the northeastern entrance to Aleppo City would have taken ten minutes. Now, with much of Aleppo in the grip of various militias and Syrian regime helicopters panning around the sky, it took a good deal longer. In many ways, the compound had made the ideal prison. It was heavily fortified with sturdy basement rooms that could easily be converted into cells; it was also right in the middle of Qadi Askar, ISIS's chosen powerbase and headquarters in Aleppo. The problem, however, was that the Islamic State militants were forced to share both the area and the compound with other rebel groups they didn't trust, and who, in turn, were growing increasingly suspicious of them.

Moving everyone out to Sheikh Najjar was a stroke of genius. Its industrial zone is as big a medium-sized city center, with grid upon grid of beige factory buildings, anonymous warehouses and heavy machinery. With dozens of basement storage facilities and easy escape eastward via a motorway to

Raqqa, it was a perfect place to keep high-value merchandise safe from prying eyes and possible theft.

Long after the foreign prisoners had departed, the Syrian army would retake the area and invite a friendly TV crew in to view the secret prison. They were entirely unaware that it had once been home to Islamic State's entire trove of Western hostages; some of those who made it out would have to find the footage on YouTube and share it among themselves. In the footage, a cameraman accompanies a flak-jacketed Syrian journalist as he walks through the underground space, strolling past tiny cells that look more like toilet cubicles. The reporter opens a metal door into another area of the prison in which larger rooms were set aside as communal holding cells, picking through detritus as he goes: blankets, clothes, plastic bottles, Islamic State propaganda in a variety of languages. *"We go to the other section of the prison. On the right. It's a very large area. It shows how big are the cells that they used to imprison the citizens of Aleppo. You can see here very rough and frightening pictures [...] You can see I don't know what these writings are; I don't know what all this is but it shows the cruelty that was used with innocent people. These people are doing all this in the name of Islam. They use God's name to justify this cruelty."*

On a journalist trip to regime-held Aleppo in the summer of 2015, I persuaded the Syrian army to take me to the same makeshift prison. Sheikh Najjar was still a military zone: the sound of incoming shells and the crackle of automatic weapons could be heard clearly on its outskirts. Many of the new-build factories and municipal buildings had been flattened or burned out; some of those still standing were still daubed with Islamic State graffiti. Presently we arrived at a mansion block where, behind a huge gate, half a dozen stony-faced pro-regime paramilitaries—the feared *shabiha*—sat pushing themselves back and forth on a communal swing in the afternoon heat. After a long wait to get permission from their commanding officer, they ambled lazily around the side of the building and opened up the grille of what looked like a lock-up garage or a shipping container. Down one flight of stairs and there, among shavings and planks of wood, was the elaborate metal latticework of the same prison door. It was a sunny day, but everything beyond was in total darkness. My hosts wouldn't let me go any further—they claimed not to have the key—but I could make out a passageway leading to another metal door which in turn led deeper into the prison; the whole cavernous area, according to one of the *shabiha*, consisted of between ten and fifteen rooms. Just inside the entrance sat a table with two chairs on either side, presumably to interrogate prisoners.

It was in this clammy basement storage space, a disused wood or furniture factory, that many of the foreign hostages would spend three or four months. Didier François remembers being put back in a room with Foley and Cantlie on October 5, 2013. The foreigners had been smuggled out in groups of two or three; on August 29, along with two others, the French journalist had been the first to arrive. "They don't tell you why they move you, and if they do they usually lie," said Didier. "There were only three of us; two French plus one other guy. In September they brought in two other French from Aleppo City, then James, John, David and Federico. Then they brought in Steve." For the first time, all the men were lumped together in a single big room. In time some of the hostages would call their time in captivity "the box"; this was the first box.

"In Sheikh Najjar, they built the prison around us," remembers François. "When we came in, there was nothing there. It was just a normal factory." The Islamic State prison builders had carefully converted the basement into two parts; the first contained fourteen single cells while the second had about a dozen more cells and three big rooms. The Western hostages' room was about five meters square, with a toilet on one side and a table on another. Conditions were much the same as in Aleppo, except that the food was less plentiful—often little more than a few olives or an egg—and the biting North Syrian winter was on its way. The place was in almost permanent darkness and so cold that some of the prisoners put down planks of wood to insulate them from the stone-cold floor.

At least in the early days, some had only the sketchiest idea of who their kidnappers were. Pierre Torres's initial kidnappers didn't tell him they were from Islamic State: "The first thing they said they were [pro-regime] *shabiha* from Deir El-Zour." Every time the guards entered the room, he and his fellow hostages were forced to kneel, cup their hands over their faces and affix themselves to the nearest wall. "They used lots of tricks to make sure we don't know who they are and where we are," said Torres. "And if they move you, even from one room to another in the same prison, they blindfold you." In ten months of captivity, during which he was passed around from group to group, the French reporter Nicolas Hénin only twice heard that he was in the hands of Islamic State. He said, "The problem is that when you are taken hostage, the people who take you will have a lot of fun by not telling you who they are. These people don't introduce themselves to their hostages."

Like many of the others, Hénin was still wearing the same

clothes he'd been captured in six months earlier, and he would continue to wear them for nearly his entire stay in Sheikh Najjar. But conditions could have been worse. While many of the journalists had been tortured or ill-treated before they arrived—including almost all the British and American men—none were in Sheikh Najjar. They were still under the overall custody of Abu Athir and Abu Obeida al-Maghrebi, but the sadistic British guards had been posted elsewhere. The prison chief in Sheikh Najjar was a French-Tunisian going by the name of Abu Mohammed al-Franci; he was more French than Tunisian, and didn't seem to know any Arabic. Then there was Abu Obeida's deputy Abu Maryam, a Syrian from near the border with Iraq whose job was to supervise the Islamic State prisons. Some of the Syrian guards were fitfully friendly to the prisoners, occasionally bringing them sweets and jam.

For Foley and Cantlie the change of location was both a blessing and a curse. In Aleppo their conversion to Islam meant they'd been treated better than everyone else. Here, with everyone in the same room, it didn't seem to matter. Their Arabic names were forgotten, as were their privileges. On the other hand, here was the chance of a little group solidarity and to get news from the outside world. Some of their fellow hostages—David Haines and Federico Motka—were already familiar to them from their time with the British guards; both looked like skeletons. Others, like the French, were new faces.

More foreign journalists and aid workers were arriving all the time, and from all over Northern Syria. Sooner or later they found their way to Sheikh Najjar and were added to the group. From the nearby suburbs of Aleppo came at least some of a Sky News Arabia team that had gone missing in October—one of

the Western hostages would overhear their Lebanese cameraman in another part of the prison. Peter Kassig would eventually be dispatched there from Raqqa, as would the two Spanish
journalists Ricardo Vilanova and Javier Espinosa, who'd been
held in the same prison. Some of the journalists arrived in
pairs; others were already friends or knew of one another from
the Syria beat. "Hello, brother," Espinosa remembers Foley
hollering when he was first ushered into the room. Ricardo
Vilanova also counted Jim Foley as a good friend. A Syrian veteran, he'd introduced Foley to his fixer Mustafa, and had been
with all three men in Aleppo City only days before Foley and
Cantlie went missing; he was shocked to see them here in such
atrocious conditions. Pierre Torres already knew Espinosa and
Vilanova too. Peter Kassig knew Steven Sotloff and was able
to tell him that their mutual friend Barak Barfi was across the
border in Antakya, working on his case. Sotloff, Kassig and
Foley had even stayed at the same chintzy Antakya hotel, the
Antik Grand, on previous trips inside.

Inevitably, conversation among the prisoners turned to
how they had been taken in the first place. Some had just
been unlucky: in the wrong place at the wrong time. Foley
and Cantlie's kidnapping had clearly been planned, but they
blamed no one but themselves. They'd grown lazy and com-
placent, and attracted attention where they should have been
trying to blend in. Steven Sotloff's abduction was no accident
either. The masked men waiting for them on the road, his Syrian guide Yosef told me later, must have been tipped off by
someone in the local rebel media office. Indeed, in the fren-
zied telephone game being played on the Syrian–Turkish border, he might well have been damned even before he arrived

in the country. A Syrian activist who Sotloff met and asked to accompany him turned him down because of the risks. "I heard a lot of rumors about him," she told me. "That he was a spy, that he was in the army, that he had a necklace that looked like a military dog tag. I heard from another person that he had two passports. So I couldn't trust him—he'll be kidnapped, I thought." Peter Kassig had begun to suspect he'd been betrayed too. "Peter was convinced that someone who he knew intimately had sold him out," said an American who debriefed some of the released European hostages. "Not someone with him on the trip, but an activist who knew when he went in and when he left. This is what they talked about day and night, him and another prisoner."

If a Syrian activist did betray Kassig to Islamic State, it might well have been someone he'd come across during his time working as a medical instructor and logistics manager for ARK, a British-led conflict research consultancy with offices in Turkey between October 2012 and June 2013. ARK (Analysis, Research, Knowledge) was in 2012 entrusted by the U.S. State Department and other Western governments with distributing "non-lethal aid" to the Syrian opposition and helping activists overthrow the regime—to act as a flier for a Western-friendly transitional government as Bashar al-Assad struggled to control the country. ARK paid Syrian activists to make propaganda videos against their regime; later it won some contracts to provide civil defense to areas of Northern Syria. Secrecy was paramount. ARK, according to an American who worked directly alongside it, was "intentionally opaque...there are almost no public documents. A lot of these characters [in ARK] come out of the post-Iraq, post-Afghanistan industry, both in the U.S.

and the UK. Many have defense backgrounds, or intelligence backgrounds."

A few of its employees were former British Army; one was recognized by the same visiting American from CIA circles in Beirut. Then there were pollsters and policy advisers, a consultant who previously worked for a "psychological operations" [PSYOPS] firm, and a development professional with experience in "in-country information-gathering." In dozens of interviews with Syrian activists about ARK, most told me they'd deliberately given it a wide berth, assuming it to be a waste of money and a front for intelligence gathering. ("You say he is an aid worker," said one early communication from the kidnappers to Kassig's family. "We know that all Westerners who say they are E.M.T's or aid workers are just spies.") Kassig didn't much like ARK either; four months before he was kidnapped he'd quit to focus on his own humanitarian missions inside Syria. Either way, and according to Kassig's sometime Syrian girlfriend who also worked for ARK, the organization panicked after his kidnapping—and instructed everyone to keep quiet about his time there.

After a while, there was little point in reviewing possible mistakes or alleged betrayals. Everyone who ventures into a war zone makes mistakes, but the hostages' misfortune was to be punished for them over and over again. In time they'd learn to spend their time more fruitfully, providing one another with entertainment and support. Daniel Rye Ottosen, a former gymnast, instituted a daily fitness and calisthenics program, putting everyone through their paces to keep their bodies from withering any further. "OK, nine o'clock: now it's time for gymnastics—who's in?" Some were, some weren't; it depended on their mood. "Steven was very down at the beginning," François told me, "but then he came back fighting." Kassig took his captivity hard too, but he fought hard to put on a brave face and helped with first aid. Foley took him under his wing, as did Sotloff and some of the others.

It was Cantlie who started the craze for chess and draughts. Edouard Elias and Didier François made a chessboard, and soon everyone was at it. "It was one of the only things that the guards would let us play," remembers François. "We were hiding it, but not too much. Some of the guards would even come and play with me." Foley inaugurated a popular series of talks, and gave lectures of his own on American literature—it had been one of his subjects at university. Sotloff was soon entertaining everyone with disquisitions on baseball and American football, and turned out to be a creative chess player: "Steven is very American," Nicolas Hénin told me, giggling at the memory. "He cheated at chess like crazy."

In the small world of Syria reporting, it was like a morbid reunion. For Foley and Cantlie it was a fillip just to find out what was happening in the world, and what was being done to get them out. To the others it must have seemed like discovering members of a long-lost tribe they had presumed would never be seen again. Every Syria journalist knew that Foley and Cantlie had been kidnapped the previous November; given the lack of real information some presumed they were already dead. The two would get tired of explaining their ordeal to each and every new arrival, but it was important for everyone to know, and now it had taken on a new urgency.

Since they were the longest-serving foreign prisoners of the Islamic State, maybe they could tell everyone else what was going on.

What could they tell them? One thing apparent to everyone in the room was that their European guards were only useful try-hards—good for translation and media work but clearly following orders from above. As had been the British who'd kidnapped Foley and Cantlie: also present that day, and clearly in charge, was a tubby, diminutive Iraqi who ran his own battalion in the Idlib countryside. "It's a very centralized, very disciplined organization," concluded François. "[The British guards] were mid-level people, and everything goes back to the top."

The "Iraqi sheikh," as Foley and Cantlie came to know him, had turned his British protégés into a small, semi-professional kidnapping team; at least some of them seem also to have been involved in the abduction of David Haines and Federico Motka four months later. He traced his support for Islamic State from long before the Syrian revolution, and claimed to have fought for the terror group Islamic State of Iraq against the American army; he even claimed to have spent several years in a U.S. military prison. Now he seemed to want to get his own back. From what Foley and Cantlie had seen he loved sweets, guns, and the ritualistic torture of Western hostages.

The breaking of nations is not a pretty sight. No one can predict who will come along to pick up the pieces. Three years earlier Islamic State of Iraq, like its parent organization al-Qaeda, had been on the ropes. The assassination of Osama bin Laden and some of its key lieutenants had thrown it into a tailspin, while the huge demonstrations of the Arab Spring sucked the air from its revolutionary ambitions. The two had always had an uncomfortable relationship anyway: Islamic State of Iraq sprang from an outfit led by a Jordanian called Abu Musab al-Zarqawi, whose brutal, monopolistic tactics and relentless slaughter of Shia Muslims was an embarrassment to al-Qaeda's leader Ayman al-Zawahiri. But when Islamic State moved into Syria, bringing weapons and expertise, another doctrinal difference emerged.

Inaugurated by a small band of jihadist veterans from Afghanistan, al-Qaeda's aim had been to build a terror organization powerful enough to take the battle to its enemies in the West, but Islamic State saw its mission as more religiously purist and more constructive: to improve the piety of Sunni Muslims and build a government around them. If al-Qaeda thrived in the chaos and the vacuum, the appearance of ISIS in spring 2013 spoke of something new—a pressing demand for the re-establishment of order.

From its new seat in Qadi Askar, one of the first things ISIS did was to send out emissaries to the poorest areas of rebel-held Aleppo, requesting that they teach their fundamentalist interpretation of the Koran and observe their puritanical strictures. From now on, they demanded, boys and girls should be separated from the age of six or seven and men prohibited from teaching girls—even if no women teachers were available. Either grateful for the protection or fearful of the consequences, the schools agreed. Other rebel groups had their own plans for the school curriculum, which largely involved keeping politics out of the classroom, but they were too busy battling the Syrian regime. "We in the opposition couldn't take taxes or build schools," a veteran Aleppo activist called Zaid Mohammed told me. "We had no central government. But ISIS were organized enough to govern an area. They took control of everything—taking taxes, paying salaries, controlling schools. The next generation is very important for their state."

Islamic State also made it a priority to close down independent politics and media and was paranoid about intelligence-gathering, but there was method and extremist principle in this madness: it stamped out crime and corruption, and the ruthlessness of its Koranic edicts applied even to its own people. Ziad Homsi, a Syrian film-maker who spent six weeks in the same Raqqa prison as Peter Kassig and two of the Spanish journalists, told me that one of his cellmates was an Islamic State fighter who'd divulged information about the group to an outsider. To atone for this indiscretion he spent most of his time praying ostentatiously, which didn't make him any new friends in the cell. Then there was a man who'd killed a child in a family dispute. When the then emir of Raqqa breezed in to take roll call, he bawled at the child-killer: "I will kill you myself in the middle of the women of the village." Many Syrians were rightly terrified of Islamic State prisons, but they were also one of the surest reasons for its support. After three years of an uprising that slid first into civil war and then into an epic regional free-for-all, Syrians of all stripes were retreating to religion, tribe and ethnic group. To some ordinary Sunni Muslims who simply wanted to live, having the Islamic State lay down the law didn't seem like a bad bet.

At the center of this bid for statehood, at least in Aleppo, was Abu Athir. Islamic State's largely medieval reading of the Koran only granted real citizenship to Sunni Muslims; everyone else was a fund-raiser. Jejoen Bontinck said that, during his time in Syria, the kidnapping of local Shia and Christians for ransom was rife: "Sometimes they asked for thirty thousand dollars, sometimes seventy thousand dollars. Sometimes their families paid, sometimes they didn't—and sometimes people got killed." When Abu Athir became governor of Aleppo, he was also handed control of its regional portfolio of prisons and the kidnapping operation; Bontinck has no doubt that his remit included foreigners. "Abu Athir would deal with ransoms. Someone he would send a letter with names saying those who should be released, including me. So he was ultimately responsible for James and John. He was ultimately responsible for everything in Aleppo."

To some extent, the new Islamic State was building on the robbery, extortion and kidnapping rackets that had long kept it afloat in Iraq; in due course kidnapping, along with the selling of oil in the areas under its control, would underpin its entire taxable economy. Almost everyone with a weapon was abducting people in Syria; Islamic State simply took kidnapping to vertiginous new heights, demanding a monopoly on everything within its areas.

The Western hostages, however, had been captured by different groups that would go on to form the nucleus of Islamic State. Foley and Cantlie and a few others were brought in by the Iraqi sheikh; the Spanish reporter Marc Marginedas was transported all the way from Hama; others were nabbed by small groups of *muhajireen*. In a few cases there'd even been attempts to work out a ransom. In summer 2013, according to two people directly involved, a team trying to secure the release of some foreign hostages were dealing with Abu Athir, Abu Obeida al-Maghrebi and an "Iraqi sheikh"—who may or may not have been the one who took Foley and Cantlie. Negotiations were at an advanced stage. Several proofs of life had been received and a ransom of around half a million dollars agreed upon—an intermediary was even ready at the border with the money—but at the last minute all communications with the kidnappers had gone dead.

At some point the local prerogative to arrest Western journalists and aid workers had given way to a new plan, which involved herding them together and dealing with them as a group. It was likely hatched around the time the foreign hostages were first brought together in July. Given the efficiency with which the four French journalists were picked up, it could have been in the making even before that. It might have been the brainchild of Abu Athir or, more likely, someone more senior in Islamic State's governing council in Iraq—perhaps even its mercurial leader Abu Bakr Baghdadi himself. To some of the hostages in that room in Sheikh Najjar, the industrial scale of the kidnapping effort might have seemed good news: it meant they were useful for something, that there would shortly be some kind of negotiation to get them out.

But then why had they hidden Jim Foley and John Cantlie away for a whole year and not bothered to try bartering them? There was something else at work here too, a showy desire to manifest power that went far beyond kidnapping for ransom. Many struggled to reconcile the new Islamic State's extravagant cruelty with its pretensions to government, but really they were both sides of the same coin. Any fledgling state needs to seize a monopoly on violence, and Islamic State made a point of using violence to put the fear of God into its enemies. Ahmad Primo, a Syrian media activist who was held in the same Aleppo compound as Foley and the others, told me that Abu Athir had personally supervised his torture at the hands of Abu Obeida. "He was cruel and depraved. I still have problems with my body from his striking." While Abu Obeida was beating Primo with sticks, Abu Athir had asked his security chief to read out the things he had written on Facebook, and then joined in the assault. "You're a journalist," he shouted. "I enjoy killing journalists."

When it came to foreign journalists, Islamic State's desire to exhibit power involved mimicking the worst excesses of its enemies. Its propaganda obsessions were Guantánamo, the war on Islam, the American occupation of Iraq. During their time with the Iraqi sheikh, Foley and Cantlie had been waterboarded—the torture technique employed by the CIA against al-Qaeda suspects. It happened several times, at least one of which followed a botched attempt to escape. "The waterboarding was not every day, maybe two three times," Jejoen told me.

And that early tip that Jim Foley had been seen standing in a jihadi prison with his arms held wide as if he were being crucified was, in retrospect, very likely a good one. The same torture would be inflicted on Foley later too; Didier François would see it with his own eyes. It's wasn't a crucifixion, but another dark parody of the war on terror: a reconstruction of the famous Abu Ghraib prison photo in which a hooded Iraqi was made to stand, arms outstretched, by American guards.

Another prisoner to arrive in Sheikh Najjar was Omar al-Khani, the Syrian boyfriend of the young American aid worker Kayla Mueller. Al-Khani had been released from the Aleppo compound in the middle of September, around the time the Western hostages were whisked away to Sheikh Najjar and almost immediately he began planning to get Mueller out. "I was looking for a way to go back to them and talk about Kayla," he told me. It wasn't long before he found one. A friend put him in touch with a senior ISIS emir in nearby Idlib Province, and al-Khani had spent three days with the man, charming him, advising him on how to use new media, begging him to intercede with Islamic State's Sharia court in Aleppo to get Mueller out. They'd stolen his girlfriend, his cameras and his money—all of which, he felt sure he could reason, was *haram* (forbidden) under their interpretation of the Koran. It was a smart pitch—holding the Islamic State to its own rules—and the emir listened patiently before advising him to write everything down in a petition to the Sharia court in Aleppo. A month passed and the call came that the judge had granted him an audience. Al-Khani duly presented himself at an Islamic State headquarters and several hours later a car came and drove him to Sheikh Najjar. It was ironic, he'd realize later: Sheikh Najjar was where he and Mueller had been kidnapped three months previously, and now he was headed there again to get her back.

If ever they were stopped by members of the Islamic State of Iraq and Sham, al-Khani had explained before he and Mueller traveled to Aleppo, she should pretend they were man and wife. The cover story might buy her protection from their strict moral code, he thought, as puritanical Islamists would hardly kidnap the visiting wife of a local Muslim. He'd whispered it again in the back of the taxi on the day they were kidnapped, and he'd written it in his long petition to the Sharia court too, but as soon as he stood in front of the Islamic State judge in Sheikh Najjar the whole story unraveled. "He said, 'I have read your letter and I believe there is some truth in it, but some of it is not true.' And then he started talking about Kayla—that she was from the United States, that she was our enemy, that I shouldn't support her. And then all this nonsense about the CIA, the FBI and spies. They make this accusation of everyone, even their own people." Al-Khani expected that to be the end of it, but the judge wasn't finished. His guards had gone to fetch Mueller, who now stood in front of him wearing a veil and a long black cloak. The judge promised her that al-Khani would not be harmed if she told the truth; was she really his wife? Al-Khani could see that, under her veil, she was crying. "No, he is not my husband. He is my fiancé," she replied. The encounter lasted only a few minutes, and it was the last time al-Khani would ever see Mueller. Now accused of lying by the judge, he was marched out of the room by masked gunmen and thrown in a cell of his own.

Al-Khani's tiny cell was only a few meters away from the room in which the Western hostages were being kept. It was dark all the time—candles were only brought when it was time for him to eat—but almost everything was audible and, peering out from under his prison door in search of Mueller, he saw signs of activity and heard people speaking English, including Jim Foley. From the sound of it, there were more than a dozen foreigners in the room, and they were not doing well. Didier François was frank about the problems posed by shared captivity. "It is not easy to be a hostage," he told me when I met him in Paris. "To be put for so long in a room with people who you didn't choose. There are different people, with different experiences and ways of looking at things, and different survival strategies. There is little food, pressure, stress. If you're tired, if you're hungry, if you're afraid—people are fighting, people are arguing."

Foreigners who gravitate to war zones—usually journalists and aid workers—are either used to being the center of attention or entirely self-possessed, attracted to the work precisely because they function better on their own. Sometimes they're both. "People who travel to these countries," reflected Pierre Torres, "are really used to be being by themselves. I'm a pure example of this. For me it's really cool and I enjoy it a lot, but we are generally really bad at being in society. So when we were forced to live together, most of us had to make a huge effort. Sometimes it worked, sometimes it failed."

There was little time for gentlemanly behavior. David Haines had suffered so many blows from the British guards that he suffered permanent digestive problems and couldn't hold food down very well. Some of the other prisoners suffered from almost continual diarrhea. One or two may have had medical and psychological problems even before they arrived. There were fights. With so many strong characters in such close quarters and in constant fear for their lives, it was only to be expected. Many of the quarrels were among those who were already good friends. "Steven and Peter were fighting and arguing all the time but they were very close," remember François. "We had some fights, me and Steven, but we got along. We're both stubborn." Moods changed, as did alliances. "It's funny because at times I was very close to some," says Nicolas Hénin, "and a bit further away from others. I had a period in which I was very close to John; and Steven was my enemy. A couple of months later it turned around, and it was the opposite." One tension that emerged was between those who want to act as a group and those who wanted to rely on their individual wits. "If I got diarrhea," says François, "I would knock on the door because I will ask to go to the toilet. Some people will think, if you knock on the door I will piss off the guards, which will not be nice. Some people wanted to take a vote. So I would say, 'Fuck you—I don't give a shit about your vote. If I want to knock on the door I will knock on the door.' It's not always easy; we don't always have the same approach."

Jim Foley became the peacemaker, preventing the bickering from degenerating into something worse. The one he himself would argue with most was, naturally, Cantlie. They were such good friends, and had been cooped up together for so long, that each knew what the other was thinking before anything was said. But they were also very different characters. Either to help boost morale or because he genuinely believed they could all make it out, Jim liked to put on a brave face. "Jim was mostly optimistic," remembers François, "though he had his ups and downs like everyone else. John was more pessimistic." It was only to be expected. Three times now he'd tried to escape from different groups of British Islamists, and each

time he'd been caught and tortured. He knew more than anyone what these people were capable of, and how difficult it was
to second-guess their view of the world. The experience seems
to have changed him, made him quieter and more withdrawn.
"Before he was all hyper and active," according to a security
source who debriefed many of the European hostages, "and
then he mellowed out. In contrast to Foley, who was optimistic, sometimes he seemed like a broken man."

By the time al-Khani arrived in November, two hostages
had emerged as leaders and interlocutors with the guards:
François, whose approach was to use charm and negotiations;
and Foley, who preferred to hustle for better conditions—more
food, more blankets, fresh clothes. The only reason al-Khani
knew Foley's name so well because he "used to sit, or sleep,
closest to the door. Because every time they bring food, or they
want to check or do anything, they would always encounter
him. Maybe he was the oldest there. He was always talking in
the name of the group, so I heard him more than anyone else."
Foley, according to François, was "one of the persons who were
not afraid of being beaten by the guards. Some people will
say don't try because it is dangerous to ask, and some will ask.
James was one of those people who were not afraid to take the
risk of asking."

Sometimes the approach seemed to work. "Once they brought
them clothes and T-shirts and stuff, and gave it to them," says
al-Khani, "and he said, 'Oh thank God, these are the first new
clothes for two years.' I remember this clearly. They were very
happy with this." It was typical of Foley, an upbeat comment
with a barb in the tail aimed at his captors, but it risked antag-
onizing them.

Sometime in late October or early November they'd brought in a Russian engineer called Sergei Gurbonov who'd been arrested by the volatile, Chechen-led *muhajireen*, some of whose fighters had migrated to Islamic State. Even before he arrived at Sheikh Najjar it was clear that he had been badly tortured; some of the others thought it had driven him a little mad. At least for him, there was no respite in Sheikh Najjar. A few times, says al-Khani, a Chechen guard took Gurbonov out of the communal cell and began talking to him in the corridor, and then punching him furiously. It was a reminder that serious mistreatment was never far away.

Abu Athir visited the prison two or three times, presumably to check up on his prisoners. Al-Khani didn't see him personally but a fellow inmate, an Egyptian former fighter for Islamic State, muttered that he was "the big guy in charge." Another thing al-Khani remembers was hearing one or two of the hostages being taken out of the cell so that the guards could talk to them privately. One masked Islamic State militant who arrived at the prison to interrogate them spoke good English as well as classical Arabic, and al-Khani concluded that he was British. Sometimes he heard the man taking down email addresses. He guessed it was to ask their families for money.

CHAPTER SIX

Dealing with the Devil

The first email was only four lines long. It arrived in the United States on November 26, 2013 via an encrypted, untraceable email account and was addressed to Michael Foley and Phil Balboni, Jim Foley's editor at *GlobalPost*. The email was written in perfect English, without capitalization and with a surprisingly emollient tone.

> hello. we have james.
> we want to negotiate for him.
> he is safe: he is our friend and we do not want to hurt
> him. we want money fast.

Coming on the heels of Jejoen Bontinck's revelations, the Foley family viewed it as another fantastic breakthrough, but they had no idea whether it was genuine. Via their campaign website they'd received many unsolicited emails offering to share Jim's whereabouts if only an advance could be forwarded to cover someone's expenses. A response, written by the family in consultation with the FBI and their private security team, was batted back. "It was carefully crafted, trying to draw them out," says Balboni; while the tone was encouraging it made clear that they needed some way of knowing their correspondents were telling the truth. The kidnappers offered to answer whichever three proof of life questions the family cared to send. Foley's skeptical brother Michael prepared three so fiendishly specific they couldn't possibly be researched on the internet.

Who was the goalkeeper of your high-school soccer team?
Who cried at your younger brother Mark's wedding?
And who died when you were eight years old?

A few days later the answers came back word perfect. Foley's father John, after what they'd been told of his early captivity by Jejoen Bontinck, was worried that Jim "wouldn't be in a condition to remember all this stuff. The questions were so obscure—particularly the goalie question."

It was likely Bontinck's return to Europe that precipitated this email communication; it was probably for the same reason that the foreigners had been moved out of Aleppo and squirrelled away in Sheikh Najjar. The Belgian cat was out of the bag, and now the kidnappers were working to regain the initiative—another sign of their growing professionalism. The email itself was only a courtesy and a confirmation. For several weeks now the Foleys had known roughly where Jim was and roughly who was holding him. Even the proof of life was just a formality—the family knew very well that he was alive. The significance of the email was a different matter. What it meant

was that, after a year of eerie, stonewalling silence, the kidnappers were finally ready to talk. "It was the biggest deal," says
John Foley.

The first detailed email setting out the kidnappers' demands
arrived a week later, on December 2. The kidnappers didn't
mention the Islamic State of Iraq and Sham; in at least one of
their emails, according to Diane Foley, they even purported to
be "a Free Syrian Army unit," which clearly wasn't true. Their
emails repeatedly warned the Foley's "to be quiet and stay
away from the media," or face dire consequences. They didn't
mention any prohibition on talking to the American government; everything the Foleys got they shared with the FBI and
anyone else in Washington who showed an interest. The FBI
didn't tell the Foleys that they couldn't pay a ransom, nor did
they play an active part in the negotiations. "They just told us
to do it and tweaked the letter," says Diane.

Each response was written by the family, with the input
of the FBI and their security team, who would occasionally
change some of the wording. The strategy—established practice within the FBI and the commercial K&R industry—was to
keep the kidnappers talking. "They really didn't want to negotiate with us; they wanted to negotiate with our government,"
is how John Foley saw it. "And they had an opportunity to
do that based on the fact that we'd given this to the FBI. But
nobody in that damn clique was willing to acknowledge that.
So they kept telling us—this is what you need to do, you need
to keep them talking, to engage them."

After Jim Foley's death news outlets reported that the ransom demanded for his release was one hundred million euros,

but that wasn't quite true.[3] The deal offered was one hundred million euros *or* unnamed "Muslim prisoners" in return for all of the British and American men in the kidnappers' possession. "I don't think it was just for Jim; I can't remember them saying too much about Jim specifically in their emails," Diane Foley told me. "I would imagine it was one hundred million for the whole lot," added her husband. Around the same time the Foleys received their email, almost identical messages went to most of the families of the British and American men, including the partner and family of John Cantlie. There was a degree of ambiguity in some of the communication, but as things progressed everything suggested that the American and British hostages were being bargained for together. The other families or their representatives who spoke to me said they contained the same ransom offer: 100 million euros.

The kidnappers were clearly trying to use that group of hostages as a bloc to force a deal, or some kind of engagement, with their real enemies—the American and British governments. When some of the European hostages were freed they also attested to this being a group deal. "It's not true, they didn't ask a hundred million euros for Foley," Didier François told me. "It's not accurate to say that. To tell you the truth, the hundred million was not for him—it was for six people, American

---

3. The source for the story that the ransom demand for Jim Foley was one hundred million euros appears to have been Phil Balboni. In a face-to-face interview in October 2014, he told me: "Some believed that there was a desire for a group negotiation. I never believed that." The weight of evidence from my interviews with the Foley family, from my interviews with security people with direct knowledge of the case, from my discussions with other representatives of American and British hostages and from my interview with Didier François, suggests that this was not the case.

and British. I know it because I was one of the people who were given the proposal; we were there in the room when they made the proposal. So we know it was not one hundred million; at least in the room it was not one hundred million. They suggested it to all the prisoners." When I put it to him that maybe the British and Americans were being treated differently, that maybe Islamic State may never have had any intention to sell them for money, he shook his head firmly. Other released French hostages said the same: Islamic State wanted money, from wherever they could find it.

Perhaps understandably, the governments didn't want to play this game. But the result was that that Jim and Diane Foley, along with the other British and American families, were forced to go through the motions of dealing with the kidnappers as private individuals, as if this were just a tussle over money. "We thought we were in a game of tennis which was going to go back and forth and back and forth many, many more times," remembers Phil Balboni. "The FBI suggested that we stall," says Diane. "Tell the truth—that you're from a middle-class family, that you don't have anything. They made it sound like we were going to have lots of opportunities to negotiate." The problem was that these weren't conventional ransom kidnappings, so the skill set of their FBI and security advisers wasn't likely to have much effect. The kidnappers' demands were really addressed to the government; the family found itself as a pawn in the middle, being used as a buffer.

It didn't work, and the tone of the kidnappers' emails went rapidly downhill. They became "very insulting," says John Foley. "They called us ants, they called us sheep, because we follow the government. Always tried to demean us—saying we were mindless followers of the government." In total the kidnappers only sent about four emails. The last arrived around a month after the first, and was both brief and threatening. "This is the last email you are going to receive from us," it said. The kidnappers had left the Foleys a punishingly tiny window in which to sort out a huge ransom. "I thought the whole thing was crap," says John Foley. "If I was holding Jimmy, all I'd want to know was 'How much money are you going to give me?' They don't care about the rest. They were getting gobbledygook from us. They got tired of hearing our bullshit." For a long time afterward the Foleys continued to fire off emails, setting out their limited finances and repeatedly making the case for Jim's return. But there was never any reply.

The families' excitement at the communication from the kidnappers was nothing in comparison to the boost it gave Foley and Cantlie. From the beginning their Islamic State kidnappers had been practiced liars. The British guards in particular had thrown up whole tissues of lies—for fun, to appease and motivate, but most importantly to humiliate and psychologically torture those who fell into their charge. The only information the hostages knew for sure wasn't being manipulated came in via the proof of life questions, which had to have come directly from their loved ones.

For the Foleys, the value of their three questions wasn't just about establishing who was holding Jim. Posing questions about intimate family memories was their way of letting him know that they were still out there, that they were thinking of him and looking for him—and doing their best to bring him home. "Now Jim knew we had found him," says Diane Foley. "And he knew that we knew he was alive. And we were so elated." To be discovered alive after such a long descent into the Islamic State's subterranean prison network must have seemed unreal. When he returned to the communal cell in Sheikh Najjar, having given his guards the proof of life answers, some of his fellow hostages saw Foley well up with emotion and collapse into tears.

The euphoria wouldn't last. It's unclear when the hostages worked out that the communication to secure their release had been aborted, but Islamic State's impatience with the Foley family wasn't just a fit of pique: circumstances had intervened, and now they had problems of their own. Their relentless empire-building had brought them into conflict with other rebel militias and, too late, the latter realized that Islamic State's goal wasn't so much about toppling the Syrian regime as sowing the seeds of their own Islamist government. The brewing hostilities probably explain why, in their correspondence with the Foleys, the kidnappers pretended to be from the Free Syrian Army. They were likely trying to blacken the reputations of the Western-friendly militias with which they were about to go to war. They didn't tell their prisoners anything, but many could guess that something was afoot. "We could hear fighting around the prison, and not far away," remembers François.

The Western hostages were finally ushered out of their basement on December 23 or 24, 2013. Their captors were in a hurry, because they were being forced out of Sheikh Najjar at gunpoint, in a deal brokered with other rebel groups. It was also the moment at which the Foleys received their final, intemperate email, putting an end to the dialogue. The day they were taken away, Omar al-Khani remembers hearing lots of activity after morning prayers, and the delivery of a change of clothes for the foreigners. Presently Abu Maryam, the Syrian in control of the Islamic State's prison system, arrived with a translator—very likely the same Brit who'd earlier been at the prison to interrogate the prisoners and ask for email addresses—to make an important announcement. "We are sorry," the pair told the assembled hostages. "It is wartime; we don't know our friend and we don't know our enemy, but we are going to release you soon. We need to make sure you will be in a secure situation, to make sure any other groups don't take you again. We will take you to the Turkish border. This trip will take two or three hours, so please be patient. You will be with your families by tonight."

It was another lie. In a deal brokered with other rebel groups, Islamic State was allowed to leave Aleppo with its entire haul of prisoners and weaponry. As it retreated from its bases in the city, Islamic State fighters left behind the bodies of dozens of Syrian activists and journalists. The order for these executions, several Aleppo rebels told me, could only have come from Abu Athir. The families and friends of the Western hostages would pore over footage of the bodies on YouTube in case they saw signs of their loved ones, but they weren't there. The foreigners were alive, but they weren't going home. Instead, they were being taken on a punishing mystery tour of Northern Syria. All were loaded onto a dank commercial lorry and added to a huge convoy of hundreds of jihadis and their families in jeeps and military vehicles. Their first stop was in the countryside of Aleppo Province, tantalizingly close to the

Turkish border. After that they'd go to Idlib, where Islamic
State had old friends, and from there they'd go south and stay
a few nights in Hama. Most of the driving was done at night.
They were blindfolded, and handcuffed to each other in pairs.

In all, the convoy would snake through four provinces. On
its final leg, which lasted for three days and nights and went
through rocky territory, it had grown to include everything
from anti-aircraft guns to bulldozers. By now there were nineteen male hostages; the women, including Kayla Mueller, were
on the same journey but in a different vehicle. On their truck
the men were only given dates to eat and had to defecate into
plastic bags. "They carried us along with their shit," remembers Nicolas Hénin. "It was a commercial truck packed with
bag of blankets, boxes of dates, and barrels of chemicals for
use in their home-made bombs. There was writing on them,
which said something like 'hazard, dangerous, acid.' We were
just sitting on these barrels of chemicals in the truck." Their
Moroccan minder was wearing a suicide belt, and cheerfully
showed them the button with which he would deploy it if the
hostages attempted to try anything. The hostages took refuge
in black humor too. "On the bright side," one murmured to
another, "everything will be pretty quick."

The rebel purge of Islamic State was successful in Aleppo,
but it proved disastrous elsewhere. ISIS returned to the city
with reinforcements led by its much-feared Chechen-led brigade of foreign fighters, and before long it was the rebels' turn
to flee. The fighting was merciless; in one of a series of massa-
cres, militants killed thirty-five members of a single rebel family, chopped up some of their body parts and threw them in a
nearby river. The assault on Islamic State's positions had added

immeasurably to the group's paranoia and concentrated the minds of its leaders on the need to establish their state. That was the reason for the crazy, circuitous route taken by the convoy. Such was the chaos enveloping Northern Syria that they were looking for somewhere they owned, which they wouldn't have to share with other rebel groups.

When the dust settled, they had it: for the first time ISIS had exclusive control of Raqqa Province. It would become the crowning glory of their new state, and where the Western hostages and the rest of their traveling jihadi circus would end up. At every stage of their journey, as Foley and Cantlie would have been the first to realize, the Iraqi sheikh was back in charge of their custody. So was his sadistic entourage of British guards.

"This American is a soldier," declaimed the Iraqi sheikh, pointing his finger at Jim Foley. "We have communicated with his government to try to negotiate a prisoner exchange. You know what they replied? They sent us an email saying, 'We won't negotiate with you even if you kidnap a thousand like him.' What do you make of that? To your own country you have no value. They would prefer us to kill you." It was a series of extravagant lies. Foley had once been embedded with American troops in Afghanistan, and the kidnappers might have found some of the photos on his computer; and there was no evidence that the kidnappers had ever been in direct communication with the American authorities. But it was also the first time the Iraqi sheikh had spoken to all the hostages together— it was one reason why Javier Espinosa would remember it.

Foley and Cantlie knew the Iraqi well from their early, brutal months of their captivity, but most of the others had no idea who he was. Whatever else his reappearance meant, it was unlikely they were going home in a hurry.

This was February 2014. The occasion for the speech was their arrival at a two-story villa overlooking the Euphrates River in Raqqa. Listening to it was a captive audience of nineteen men, sitting handcuffed in pairs and packed into a single room. In the next room was Kayla Mueller and a number of other women, including three continental Europeans from Medécins Sans Frontières (MSF) and a woman who had been abducted while working for the Red Cross, assessing the medical situation in Idlib the previous October. Little is known about the former, all of whom were eventually released and presumably sworn to secrecy; the latter, an older woman, was a hugely respected aid worker and veteran of many of the world's worst trouble spots, and with whom the young Kayla Mueller appears to have formed a close bond.

The arrival of the MSF crew—there were two men as well as the three women—swelled the number of hostages considerably; they'd been abducted just a month previously, in early January, near Syria's Mediterranean coast, before being transported hundreds of kilometers to Raqqa. It was another sign of the scale of the Islamic State kidnapping operation, and the efficiency of its work. Along the way they'd also picked up a middle-aged British taxi driver called Alan Henning, who, a few days after Christmas, had driven an ambulance into Syria as part of an aid convoy and had been arrested by Islamic State almost as soon as he arrived.

As usual the newcomers were pumped for information

about the outside world. Some of the prisoners wanted to know about American foreign policy, others about football. Everyone was keen to hear about the chilling, discomfiting rise of Islamic State.

Their stay in the villa would only be for two weeks; at least in terms of its location, it was one of the most pleasant. The building was spacious, with large windows; for the first time in as long as they could remember Foley and Cantlie could see sunlight. From their vantage point they looked out over the gargantuan beauty of the Euphrates, with its epic mists and luminescent sunsets. They could see local fishermen out at work in small boats, or farmers tilling their land and tending their livestock. It was something to do, just to look.

The snag was that the preening Iraqi sheikh and his British kidnapping team seemed to have moved in too. The number of British guards grew; their boyish absurdity, coupled with their tendency to hang together as an English-speaking gaggle, earned them the nickname "The Beatles" among the hostages. Their ringleader was George, whose *kunya* some of the hostages remember as Abu Muharib ("the fighter"). He was also the most religious—he spent much of his time regurgitating chunks of the Koran and had done *da'wah* in Syria. Then there was an Abu Jihad. The masked jihadi who was there the day Foley and Cantlie were kidnapped and who eventually appeared in the execution videos was John, or Abu Saleh ("the pious one"). John seemed smarter than George, who was considered very dim. According to Jejoen Bontinck and another freed hostage, Foley mentioned another Brit who called himself Abu Osama, the man had been there early in his captivity and had "treated him well," but they hadn't seen him again.

In February 2015 the *Washington Post* identified John as Mohammed Emwazi, a Briton from a Kuwaiti background who'd already been in trouble with the police and the security services in Britain, and who disappeared from his west London home in late 2012. At around the same time, Choukri Ellekhlifi, a British jihadi from the same London school, skipped bail after being convicted of street robberies and also headed for Syria. Since they were sighted in the same areas it's possible the two went together or joined up soon after they arrived. Ellekhlifi was killed in the summer of 2013. A video passed to me at the time showed him and some friends diligently performing *da'wah* on the streets of Edgware Road in west London a few months before he went. His chosen nom de guerre, according to an internet profile he left behind, was Abu Osama.

By now there were a full complement of four Beatles; they made one of the rooms in the villa their headquarters, and returned to the work of persecuting hostages as if they'd never been away. George, the leader, usually arrived with John and Ringo; Paul was around much less, and dropped in and out of the group. So pungently distinctive was the smell of George's cheap aftershave that the prisoners knew he was on the way before he arrived. He was also the most gratuitously cruel and, perhaps following the lead of the Iraqi, he hated Jim Foley more than any of the others. All of them seemed to relish making an example of the unfortunate American, using him to warn the others about the perils of falling out of line. "Explain what waterboarding is," Javier remembers one saying. "James, tell the dogs what happens if you try to escape from here!"

Many of the hostages had been forced to don orange Guantánamo-style jumpsuits. The prospect of ending up in an orange jumpsuit was exactly why Cantlie had tried to bolt the first time he'd been held by British Islamists. He didn't want to end up reading a prepared statement in some gory propaganda video. In one of the prisons they'd been in on the way to Raqqa, one of the others had noticed a video production room. It suggested that their kidnappers were gearing up to make films—another echo of everyone's worst nightmare, the televised beheadings of foreigners that al-Qaeda in Iraq had made its signature communication a decade earlier. Together with the appearance of a sinister Iraqi who boasted of serving under Abu Musab al-Zarqawi, it was putting everyone on edge. And, just in case anyone was minded to try another escape, they were told, a sniper had been billeted on the roof.

Islamic State now had a total of twenty-four Western hostages to play with, and its leaders were growing increasingly aware of their prize. From now on the prisoners would regularly be passed around, always blindfolded, from prison to makeshift prison. So many governments, agencies and individuals were looking for them, asking questions at the Turkish border and trying to buy influence, that they needed to be careful. There was always the risk that a greedy guard would be tempted to sell the hostages or their whereabouts for personal gain. Even an airborne rescue mission wasn't out of the question. It was why they'd been gathered in Raqqa. Some of the hostages had been held there before; they would even return to some of the same prisons. The difference now was that the city and its surrounding province were now under the complete control of Islamic State.

If the hostages' view over Raqqa looked peaceable enough, that might have had something to do with its iron rule. With

Raqqa as its base and its prototypical state, ISIS wasted no time furthering its ambitions. Deploying battle-hardened Iraqis and Chechens, the group redoubled its efforts to take full control of Eastern Syria. Annexing some of the country's most lucrative oilfields, buying off local tribes and slaughtering other rebels or soliciting their loyalty as they went, the result was a grab for land and resources the likes of which no one had foreseen. Some locals took to calling them *Da'esh*, an irreverent play on their Arabic acronym;[4] with their black balaclavas and showy use of swords, others just called them ninjas.

Among impoverished Sunni Muslims they weren't entirely unpopular; some fled the mayhem of Syria's other big cities for the safety and relative security of the Islamic State. Just as they'd done in Aleppo, they moved quickly to distribute services to citizens and charity to needy families in Raqqa. They cut down trees, organized road repairs and secured electricity for their citizens. They took a firm line on price gouging and criminality; in Raqqa they even opened a consumer protection office. Inculcating children was central. At its regular *da'wah* meetings, children's entertainment often took center stage. One propaganda picture showed its logo atop a bouncy castle. Their overarching mission was to have everyone play by their rules, to engage with their new state. "In territory controlled by the Free Syrian Army there are no rules," a veteran Syrian

---

4. The nickname Da'esh comes from a loose acronym for The Islamic State of Iraq and Sham's Arabic name, Dawlat al-Islamiya al-Iraq al-Sham, where the E stands for the 'Ayn of Iraq and the SH stands from Sham, or Greater Syria. Partly because of the Arabic meanings, it always has a negative connotation and is used only by the enemies of the Islamic State. For a more detailed explanation, see the website of Pieter van Ostaeyen at https://pietervanostaeyen .wordpress.com/2014/02/18/on-the-origin-of-the-name-daesh-the-islamic -state-in-iraq-and-as-sham/

activist called Hamza Sattouf told me. "Their system is Sharia. Even if it is bad in some things, the fact that they have one is good. At least everyone knows the rules."

Syria was now an orphan country, and a ragtag Islamist diaspora had arrived to present themselves as foster parents. The protection of Islamic State, however, came with a social contract brooking no dissent. Armed opponents, or anyone they identified as "apostates" or unbelievers, were regularly beheaded, or crucified after being killed, and their remains left to rot in public thoroughfares as a warning to others. An edict ordering Christians to pay a tax on non-Muslims (*jizya*) was largely rhetorical;[5] most had already fled. Now ISIS wasn't just another militia, but a government with powers of arrest—and after oil sales, systematic arrests were still one of their leading sources of wealth.

"Kidnapping is only one of the industries they're involved in," Pierre Torres told me. "They also control the oil, the wheat et cetera. And most of the money they make from kidnapping is smaller amounts of money taken from Syrians. But considering the numbers it makes them a lot of money. And if someone smokes or plays music, they arrest him and take money too. It's a major source of income." For most of the other groups, taking hostages was only about raising money. The Islamic State needed money too, but even here payment followed as punishment for flouting its arcane rules.

The West's failure to understand the basis of the Islamic State

---

5. *Jizya*, a per capita tax on non-Muslims, is mentioned in the Koran and justified according to some strict interpretations of Islam as a fee in return for the protection of Muslims in an Islamic State. Most Muslims, however, reject it as ahistorical and discriminatory. In ISIS's Syria territory its operation appears to have been indistinguishable from a protection racket.

and the reasons for its meteoric rise left everyone unprepared for what came next. Early on in the hostages' captivity as a group, the part-time Beatle Paul had struggled to find religious justification for their detention and shuffled off to bend the ear of the Iraqi sheikh. The Iraqi, he came back to report to Javier and a few others, had replied with an obscure Koranic authority: "He told me: you are here for having ventured into an Islamic state without an invitation. An infidel can only visit the land of Islam if your country has a pact with the Islamic state or has been invited by a Muslim." For his part, George was always whining about how much his prisoners were costing to feed and clothe. "Do you know how many bullets you could buy with the food that we give you? We're tired of you!" But he also knew that they were about to earn their keep. The Westerners had broken their rules, and it was going to cost someone a great deal to get them back.

This message is to inform you that we have taken the [country] citizen [full name of hostage] prisoner. It's very simple—a cash payment will secure his release. If you want to confirm we are really the ones holding [name] we will accept three questions from his family of a personal nature, that only he could possibly answer correctly. The conditions of [name] safe return are no media involvement whatsoever and a cash payment. Reply fast with clearly written email messages to this email address and no attachment. Act fast so as not to endanger the safety of [name].

Shortly after Jim Foley was asked for email addresses so the Islamic State could make demands of his loved ones in the Autumn of 2013, some of the European hostages had been asked for the same. Those requests began in the Sheikh Najjar prison and continued at the villa in Raqqa. All the messages were very similar to those received by the Foleys. A sample is above; it is undeniably the work of an English-speaker, almost certainly one of the Beatles. The kidnappers were canny enough to use encrypted email addresses, and to forbid the use of attachments which could be used to infect their computers and track their location. They appear to have used the same "safe" internet platform for encrypted email, and set up a fresh email account for each hostage. Given the number of hostages, the need to send secure messages and to manage each reply individually, it was no easy task. Messages would continue to arrive in the inboxes of the hostages' families until February 2014, including those of some of the Americans and British. In general, however, they seem to have judged the British and Americans too complicated and time-consuming to bother with—in any case, their governments had laws prohibiting the payment of ransoms to terrorists—and instead focused on the rest of the Europeans.

By the time the replies began to come back, the hostages had been moved again. This time they were taken to an isolated house west of Raqqa city, in an oil-rich, desert area near a town called Mansoura and a huge dam that had been built in the 1980s. Their new prison was run by North Africans, who turned out to be more humane hosts than the Beatles. Only in the prisons in Raqqa Province, remembers Didier François drily, "did they decide to feed us." In Sheikh Najjar they'd been half starved; when they were fed chicken and chips on their first day at the villa, their starved stomachs couldn't cope, which brought on another bout of diarrhea. Now, at Mansoura, they were getting used to a diet of lentils, tomatoes, boiled eggs and even fruit and tea.

Their stench had been terrible—George reveled in telling them they stank like pigs—and they'd been infested with lice; now, for the first time in months, they were allowed to take a shower. They were also brought new civilian clothes which, at least for a time, meant they could discard their sinister orange prison garb. So poor was their physical condition that a doctor was found to come and give them a look over; he gave them vitamins and calcium in an effort to bring them back to health. It was long overdue. Weakened by malnutrition, Federico Motka had problems with his teeth. Alan Henning had back problems, and was brought painkillers. Everyone was prescribed a cream to rid them of their lice and other mites.

Under the new regime, they even began to put on weight. Some turned water bottles into makeshift weights, as Cantlie had done in the Aleppo compound. At other times they read, or just talked among themselves. Didier François shared his experience of reporting the war in Chechnya. Peter Kassig taught techniques for hunting and fishing. Cantlie explained to them what it was like to pilot small airplanes. Javier Espinosa treated everyone to lectures on the counter-cultural turn in recent Spanish history, and Pierre Torres shared the secrets of iron forgery. Other impromptu classes covered everything from sailing to gourmet cookery. For the most part Jim Foley remained the convenor, but he was also a student. He already had some Spanish; now he benefited from a refresher course in the language from the Spanish speakers in the group. In a possible snub to the maniacal monotheism of his jailers, Steven Sotloff taught yoga.

Most of all, they waited. The sudden urge to feed them up and find them a doctor, some of them surmised, may not have been unrelated to the kidnappers' growing appreciation of their value, and to the fact that they were about to try selling them for huge sums of money. Javier Espinosa remembers the arrival of the messages from their families as "moments of incredible emotion" among the hostages. It made them almost look forward to the arrival of the Beatles who brought them, even though it was usually accompanied by a beating; on his turn to answer their proof of life questions, Espinosa was so nervous he momentarily forgot the name of his cousin. There were differences of opinion among the prisoners as to who was running all this. Were the Beatles just writing the ransom emails, or were they also involved in managing the process and setting the prices?

The Beatles were intimately involved in the process. "They were interested in money from the very beginning," one source who debriefed some of the hostages told me. "All thought they could retire to Kuwait or Qatar with the money they made for the ransoms. They talked about this to the prisoners, and said this in conversations amongst each other." It's likely that they were joking about making off with the money, but it was clear that they enormously enjoyed the process of extorting their fellow Europeans. The hostage for whom negotiations were most advanced, everyone in the room knew, was Marc Marginedas, a Spanish reporter. When the day came for his release the hostages stood up to say their goodbyes. Like many who followed, the reporter was heavy with messages from those who'd been left behind; almost all the hostages were allowed to send letters home to their families, but not Jim Foley. Just as Marginedas was leaving, George shouted in his direction: "Touch him, Foley. That's as close you'll ever get to freedom!" Undaunted, Foley embraced the reporter warmly anyway, and then he was gone.

Sergei Gurbonov, the Russian engineer, never managed to give the kidnappers a working email address—either that or they didn't get the reply they wanted. The beatings and mistreatment he'd suffered at their hands seem to have left him unbalanced. He spent a lot of time hiding under a blanket, laughing incessantly to himself. In any case he only spoke a little English and no Arabic. He communicated to some that he had family in Syria, but it wasn't obvious what he was doing there, or exactly when and how he'd come to be kidnapped.

In the first week of March, a few days after the release of Marc Marginedas, the Beatles showed up to take Gurbonov away. He was going to be freed too, they said. The next time they saw the Russian, it was in a close-up picture of his face, with two bullets in his forehead. George took great pride in showing the other prisoners what remained of his head. "The sheikh shot him with an explosive bullet," he boasted. The Russian had been killed, according to the Beatles, because Marginedas had ignored their instructions not to talk to the media on his return. "It wasn't true," says Didier François. "It was not the reason why they did it. The fuck who invented it was one of the British Beatles. It was just a threat to the others. He was simply preparing the ones who were due to leave to tell them not to speak to the press." The remaining prisoners organized an informal wake. Cantlie spoke up first, and then everyone else chimed in to pay their own tribute. One of the things they remembered was that he played an excellent game of chess.

If Gurbonov's death served as a warning to the others not to talk about the Islamic State's campaign of mass kidnapping if they made it out, there was also a more pressing reason for his execution, which the others couldn't have known at the time. The same horrible picture of Gurbonov shown to the hostages was immediately emailed to most, if not all, of the Europeans with whom the kidnappers were in active negotiation. He was shot, says Nicolas Hénin, "to put pressure on the negotiation. Just to show the other negotiators—OK, so this is what will happen to your fellow citizens if we do not reach an agreement with you." It was a chilling insight into Islamic State's strategic play. Even if its hostages couldn't be sold for money, they could always come in handy for something else.

The release of Marc Marginedas marked a further deterioration in the relationship between the hostages and the Beatles. They now arrived only intermittently in the prison, but went on the rampage with threats and violence as soon as they did. As usual their preferred target was Jim Foley. At one point they grabbed him by the throat so fiercely that Foley fainted and fell awkwardly, leaving him with bruising and a huge black eye. "They did it in front of me," François told me. "He was very badly hurt. It was not a holiday camp."

The violence was accompanied by a renewed interest among their North African guards in spreading Islam among their prisoners. Books and other reading materials propagating Islamic State's literal, by-the-book interpretation of Islam were delivered to their cell; some of the prisoners felt obliged to have a flick through them. The guards spent much of their time listening to recordings of prayers or lectures by clerics whose impassioned homilies would often end in tears of ecstasy. The approach of the Beatles stood out, and was more troubling. The hostages were treated to interminable rants about Koranic prophecies, about angels and demons, about an epic battle that would shortly separate believers from unbelievers and put everything right. It was exactly the same end-of-the-world show that Cantlie had endured the first time he'd been picked up by British jihadis in Syria, and it soon began to grate on everyone in the room.

The Beatles' ideas had almost certainly been picked up in fringe Koranic reading groups or treatment centers in London, and their effect in war-ravaged Syria was predictable. Witch-hunting in the Islamic State would become common, while in Raqqa masked enforcers set about beheading magicians and anyone whose amulets or superstitions left them open to accusations of witchcraft or sorcery. In the nerve-racking prison network *jinns*—invisible spirits that attach themselves to human beings—could pop up anywhere, offering an answer for anything, and sometimes needed to be driven out by force. A young Danish aid worker called Ahmad Khalid Rashidi, who spent time in Islamic State prisons in Syria, told me that his guards, too, found dark forces at work everywhere. When I visited him in Aarhus he remembered one war-damaged fellow prisoner, an American jihadi, who'd begun raving against everyone in the cell: "He has demons," the man in charge shrugged. A Shia Muslim who was held with Didier François early in his captivity howled with such ferocity after prolonged torture that the guards dragged him out of the cell and cut his head off, explaining that he was "possessed by the devil."

The hostages found different ways to survive the horror story being played out around them. On the second day of his captivity, Javier Espinosa decided to ask the guards how to pray. "The decision was inspired by the survival instinct," he wrote after his release, "but it would eventually become one of the few positive outcomes of the kidnapping. It became one of my only moments of relaxation." At around the same time, Peter Kassig converted to Islam and took the Arabic name Abdul Rahman. Peter learned his faith from an imprisoned cleric who was also a leader of Jabhat al-Nusra, but it appears to have been heartfelt. "However it came about," said a close friend of his who discussed Kassig's conversion with some of the freed hostages, "from what I know about Peter I think it became a really important part of his life. Peter was a curious guy—I think that he was interested in trying to do things. And I think that Islam is a good spiritual practice when you're in a rough situation."

Steven Sotloff's compromise with his conditions was more complicated. "Steven was praying with the guys, the Muslims," François told me, "praying as they were praying as a Muslim. Except that he would always turn thirty degrees to the West, so I think he will face the Wailing Wall rather than Mecca. I don't know if everyone knew that at the time, but I knew it." In Sheikh Najjar he'd quietly observed the Yom Kippur fast by feigning an upset stomach; François was one of those who kept his rations for him. "I kept his eggs. We had eggs that day, and eggs were very important food to keep. He didn't say he was doing Yom Kippur to the other ones, only to two people, to John and me. Because I saw him doing it. I said, 'Are you doing Kippur?' And he said, 'How do you know?' "

Jim Foley was a practicing Catholic when he arrived in captivity. When he'd been kidnapped in Libya he'd prayed the rosary. Any evidence about the authenticity of his conversion to Islam that came from Jejoen Bontinck was meaningless. To Foley and Cantlie, Bontinck was still a jihadi, and they were less than forthright about other things in the time they spent with him. On the basis on their prison conversations, François was sure that Foley's conversion was a "deliberate strategy" he adopted early on. "I'm going to tell what he asked me to tell his mother," François said. "He was deeply religious, a strong believer. It was important [for him] to pray; the only way to keep his relationship with God was to convert. He was still praying to the same God, to the same faith—there was no difference. Religion was a strong part of him, important for him—and important for his relationship to his mother. And his way to protect that and to keep it going was to convert. That's what he said, and that's what I told his mother. And she understood very well—she knows him."

It wasn't the first time John Cantlie had mulled over a conversion to Islam. During his captivity at the hands of British Islamists in 2012 he'd been invited to embrace their faith, but had baulked at the prospect. One, who the journalists labeled "Doc Junior," "asked if I was interested in converting," Cantlie wrote afterward. "By now, Jeroen and I would have said anything. My attitude was 'Yeah, of course.' Doc Junior talked it through. 'You have to believe in your heart 100 per cent in Allah.' I find the peace, gentleness and hospitality of Islam immensely appealing. But these were jihadists. No deal." Faking a conversion to Islam now, while surrounded by ferociously devout and extremely suspicious prison guards, might have seemed like a fool's errand. "If you are in that environment with these people and you make a deliberate decision to convert," one security man who debriefed some of the European hostages told me, "you go all in, you have to—otherwise you're a fucking idiot." From what Nicolas Hénin saw in the prison, and by the time he met both Foley and Cantlie, their conversion certainly seemed sincere. "I don't think they were playing a game. They had a terrible time. They were just about to die several times; they needed something to believe in."

Was the conversion of Foley and Cantlie to Islam chosen freely? It's possible that what started as a strategy gave way, as for Espinosa, to something more like solace. At the end of my conversation about prison conversions with Peter Kassig's close friend I asked him about Jim Foley and he threw the question back at me. "Have you ever tried to pray regularly? Done something five times a day for a very long period of time, repeating it at the same time and doing the same motions. There's a reason why rituals exist; there's something about the act which has powerful meaning. I think it's really hard to engage in a spiritual practice and not be affected by it. Us on the outside, what do we call that? Ultimately you're asking about the religious psychology of individuals who are facing trauma." When I spoke to Diane Foley, she broadly concurred: "I think Jim was a very spiritual person. I doubt if he totally became a Muslim. Maybe he did, but I feel Jim definitely believed in God. Whether he was a Muslim or Christian he welcomed those five periods a day where he was allowed to pray. And I know he prayed. And that's what gave him huge strength—his prayer and the prayer of some of the others." It was as good an answer as any.

Whatever Foley and Cantlie's relationship with Islam, it didn't do them much good. It had led to better treatment in the Aleppo compound, but that was only for a few months. The British guards they spent time with before and afterward didn't believe it, and by the time they arrived in Raqqa it no longer mattered. While some of their local Syrian guards along the way were more respectful of prison conversions, the British weren't. "Even among the captors many of them didn't believe in this conversion," says Nicolas Hénin. "The important ones, the British ones who will decide, they simply didn't believe it." In any case, religion was used by the foreign jihadis for largely punitive means. One of the North African guards, Javier remembers, took a vicious kick at Marc Marginedas simply for wandering past the spot where another of the hostages was prostrating himself in prayer. Federico Motka was beaten just for having a tattoo of a Buddhist symbol. The North Africans guards seemed genuinely keen to get some Islam going among their Western prisoners, but they weren't in charge—and the British, who were more powerful, never did. They were less interested in proselytizing than in using religion as another instrument with which to taunt and psychologically torture the infidels who'd fallen into their hands. "They didn't want us to be Muslims," concluded Pierre Torres, "because it wouldn't be convenient to deal with us after that."

More beneficial than conversions was whether the guards were on good terms with the prisoners and whether they thought they could be useful for anything. The eccentric

German Toni Neukirch seems to have been treated consistently better than everyone else, less because of his conversion to Islam and more because the guards simply liked him. "Once, while they were executing someone," a source who interviewed some of the hostages told me, "[the prisoners were instructed to watch and] Toni stepped on their flag. Now most prisoners would have been killed for that, but they just rolled their eyes—as if to say 'that's just Toni.'"

The week Marc Marginedas was released and Sergei Gurbonov killed I met up with Steven Sotloff's Syrian helper Yosef, who'd briefly been kidnapped with him at the Turkish border. Yosef was just back from a fact-finding mission in Syria, armed with photos of the missing secreted on his mobile phone. By then he was working with Barak Barfi to try to locate the hostages. The interesting information, he told me, was all coming from Syrians who'd been held in the "wood factory in Sheikh Najjar." Once again it was too late—both Islamic State and its foreign hostages had already been moved on. On his release from Sheikh Najjar, Omar al-Khani had passed on to the families everything they needed to know. "From the part of the prison where the foreigners were," he told me, "all of the Syrian prisoners were killed. I am the only one who got out." But Yosef had come across something else of possible interest: another Syrian had been freed from the wood factory, and he recalled hearing a guard shouting "Mon Didier"; Yosef wanted to know if the name meant anything to me.

When I ran the name past Didier François in Paris, he recognized it immediately. "OK, so they decided that I was the emir of the group, the contact person. At the end of the day I was the one knocking on the door asking for things. And when he was coming to the cell one of the French guards was always screaming *'Mon petit Didier.'* " Perhaps because of his age and experience some of the European guards liked François, and seem to have respected him—at least more than they did the other prisoners. Like Foley, François had become an interlocutor, dealing with relationships between the prisoners and the guards on a daily basis. But they also sought out and valued his advice. "They trusted Didier," says Diane Foley. "I think the captors felt that he was qualified or believable enough to give whatever information they gave him, that he would be listened to. I think at one point Didier even helped the captors to figure out what to do with the prisoners. How do you negotiate, how do you get money for them."

When it came time for the French to leave in the middle of April, François was given a secret email address. "It was whispered into his ear by the captors," said one of the other French. "They wanted it to be given only to the families." Still, even their affection for François had its limits. Before he left, they broke his finger.

There was an unsettling paradox at the heart of Islamic State's efforts to sell off its foreign hostages. The kidnappers sought direct contact with their families, which is why it needed those email addresses. But it was equally clear, as the deals were done and the hostages came out, that they were being worked through in batches according to their nation of origin or the organizations for which they worked.

Marc Marginedas had been released first, at the beginning

of March, followed by the other two Spaniards a month later; the four French were out three weeks after that, in mid-April, and the five MSF workers arrived back in two batches, in April and May. Given the efficiency with which all this was working, it was obvious that European governments and non-governmental organizations were paying up.

In fact, they'd moved very quickly to take control of the negotiations; on the other side of most of those email communications weren't families at all but rather hostage rescue specialists, spies and government agents. "The government had to pretend they were the families," one of the freed French told me. "The negotiations for our release were via an email address which was supposed to be the email address of my wife. The negotiator on the French side was sending emails with my wife's name, letting the captors believe that they were dealing with my wife—and letting them believe that four families were raising private money. As long as I was inside, the kidnappers pretended that they wanted to deal directly with families. They were happy to deal only with families. That's what they pretended."

At the end of the process, a security source who was directly involved in some of the negotiations told me, forty million euros had been handed over by European governments, NGOs and one or two families to secure the release of fifteen hostages—ten million euros of which was paid for the four French. That put the average life of each hostage at nearly three million euros; in some cases penalties or fees had also been added on for late payment.

When I spoke to Didier François he was unimpressed by speculation in the American and British media about ransoms paid by the French government. "It's bullshit. Even within the security apparatus, most people don't know. In France, including the President, no more than ten people actually know exactly what happened." One thing he was sure about was that his government hadn't handed over any money. "No, my government didn't pay," he told me. On their release, François Hollande looked all four freed hostages in the eye and told them the same thing. There was no reason to disbelieve him, but it was also clear that someone must have paid on the French government's behalf. In an interview in Paris an employee of the influential NGO Reporters Without Borders told me his best guess was that a Qatari businessman or other organization with links to the Qatari government acted as a "cut out" to pay for the French.

But it was only a guess. A security source familiar with Syria speculated that the French might have sent the money with one of the Qatari or Saudi "bag men" who go back and forth into rebel-held Syria to dole out funding to rebel groups. François was happy to admit that the French government had negotiated with Islamic State, but thought it safer that the details were best kept private. "The first responsibility is to protect our sources. This is my position as a journalist and a citizen. We are not hiding it. We do negotiate. What you do in the negotiation—is it of any value apart [from to the kidnappers]?"

It amounted to a claim of commercial confidentiality, and it was by no means unique to the French. In one case the money was handed over in a bag to a masked man on the Turkish–Syrian border. It is hard to draw any other conclusion than that MSF paid up, too: "I would have to conclude that that was the means that secured their release," said Phil Balboni. "Given everything that we know, it would be hard to imagine that they could be released in any other way." The money handed over "was comparable to the amounts paid for the others," one well-informed security man told me. "The relief of seeing our colleagues return safely," said MSF's international president upon the release of its staff, "is mixed with anger in the face of this cynical act that has cut off an already war ravaged population from desperately needed assistance. The direct consequence of taking humanitarian staff is a reduction in lifesaving aid." It's possible that any ransom paid to Islamic State came directly from funds allocated to treat wounded Syrians.

It was a fraught choice for anyone to make, and one with lives at stake on either side. The best estimates are that, in barely three months, around forty million euros had been handed over by European governments and NGOs to the world's newest and most formidable terror franchise—money that would certainly be spent on arms to help it kill, torture and control local populations in Syria and Iraq. In an echo of the information blackout insisted upon by the Islamic State and encouraged by many Western governments in relation to the kidnappings, everything was done in conditions of absolute secrecy.

Even some of those released had no idea what was given for their freedom. "There must have been some deal," Pierre Torres said to me; all he knew for sure was that nothing was handed over by his family. The Foleys told me that MSF didn't contact them to offer their help—"MSF are not very sharey," said a representative of one of the other families. Many of the hostages did their best to pass what information they had to those who needed it, but the instinct of each government and organization seemed to be to sit on the intelligence it had—and to encourage their freed hostages to do likewise. They wanted to get their own people out, and to hell with everyone else. To those outside the process, it was an eye opener as to how international relations work.

That included the families of the British and American hostages. Diane and John Foley were seeing news of freed Islamic State hostages on TV like everyone else, and it took them some time to piece together what was going on. When the Spanish arrived back, Diane Foley was desperate to find out what they knew and how exactly they'd made it out. She sent emails to the FBI and the State Department asking for help, she says, but got no reply. In the end, after one of the freed journalists got in touch, she simply got on a plane and met two of them in Barcelona. The Spanish government refused to speak to her, she says. No one wanted to talk about money, least of all the hostages whose government had helped to get them back. The French hostage experts were happy to meet her, but they couldn't say very much because their journalists weren't yet home. They did, however, voice surprise that the Foleys were dealing with this effectively alone. "The other countries used the front of the family," fumes Diane Foley. "We were the only country where the actual families wrote letters back. And they were like—*what?*"

Then came the release of the French hostages, and something more like confusion and anger. Didier François had come back bearing an email address to be given directly to the British and American families. It wasn't clear why the kidnappers wanted another direct line; they already *had* their email

addresses. Maybe they realized that they'd been communicating with spooks all long, or maybe they felt that governments
were pulling the strings of the families and they wanted the
opportunity to talk more privately. Whatever the intention,
it soon fell through the cracks of bureaucratic in-fighting
between France and the United States. "They wanted Didier to
be the messenger," is how John Foley explains it. "And Didier
is smart enough to know that he didn't want to be the sole
negotiator with the United States. So he gave the information
to the French government. The United States did not engage
with the French government."

The FBI kept telling the family that François was being
uncooperative, but that didn't sound right to the Foleys: he
seemed extremely cooperative when they talked to him.
François was happy to talk to the Foleys privately, but he also
wanted the U.S. to engage his own government. "Didier's point
was that he was very willing to help, but that he wanted it to
be done through our governments, for the U.S. to engage with
the French. He didn't want to go out on a limb himself." The
Foleys don't blame François; he was as frustrated as they were.
It was simply a disconnect between the two governments.

The email address might well have been a red herring, or a
symbol of everything else that went wrong. It would have been
easy for it to slip out, after all, or for the families to get back in
touch with the kidnappers via the encrypted email addresses
they already had. "There already were email communications," said a representative of one of the other American families, "and there was no reason to think they weren't working.
I don't know why people were fixating on that. It ultimately

came down to a disagreement between France and America. I'm not sure which side is to blame." It might even have been another torturous ploy on the part of Islamic State, designed to wreak maximum havoc and distrust among their many enemies and to offer nothing in return.

There was certainly larger politicking at work here, and on all sides. Islamic State wanted money, but equally important for its self-image as a new country was the opportunity to engage on a state-to-state level with the Western nations it most despised. Its idea for a new line to the families might have been no more than a way to bully them into applying new pressure to their governments. The American and British had long been trying to draw lines in the sand prohibiting the payment of ransoms to terrorists, and they were putting pressure on others to do the same. Given their very different policies on how to respond to kidnapping for ransom, considerable animus appears to have grown up between the French security services and their British and Americans counterparts. If the Americans were reluctant to engage with François, that might have been because they saw it as an attempt to force them into dealing with Islamic State via the French—the very last thing they would have wanted to do.

It was a complicated business, and the families were caught in the middle. But one thing was certain: whatever its interest in emailing the families privately, Islamic State categorized its hostages according to their countries of origin, and wanted to negotiate for them as such. "How many countries got their citizens out one by one?" one family representative asked me. "Did France get them out one by one or as a group? I think when we saw the other people coming out, that there was a process for getting them out, we should have done the same. I don't know if it would have worked, but it would have been interesting to try."

The next hostage to make it out, at the end of May, was the aid worker Federico Motka. He was the only Italian held by Islamic State, and the multi-million euro deal was brokered by the same Italian secret services agency that had negotiated the release of Domenico Quirico the previous September. Among the dwindling number of hostages Motka had said goodbye to was David Haines, his British co-worker who'd been abducted with him more than a year earlier. They'd been through hell together, especially in those early months when they joined Foley and Cantlie in the custody of the Beatles. Now one was going home to his family, and the other was staying put.

For those left behind it was the cruelest possible illustration of the different life chances of those whose countries did negotiate with Islamic State and those, from Britain and the United States, which refused to do so. As more hostages went home, those left behind became painfully aware that there were now two different categories of prisoner; it added to the tension in the room. "Maybe, if only subconsciously," a representative of one of the American families told me, "they knew that their fate was linked to their government's decisions. I think people were afraid of being associated with the Americans and the British."

Many of the Europeans knew that their governments would try everything to get them out. "I had a good understanding of what my government was doing and how they were doing it," François told me. "It's very easy when you have that certainty. I knew my job was to survive and get through it. That's easy. It's a straight line, and you keep your eyes on the objective. When you don't—when you're not sure, you're discussing, you're adopting, you keep analyzing, it goes on and on. You have ups and downs, because you don't know—you hope, you despair. That is much, much more difficult."

One thing keeping up the spirits of the Brits and Americans was brutal logic. Why would their kidnappers keep them alive for so long, at such expense in manpower and resources, only to kill them at the end of it? "We had this discussion for hours and hours and hours while we were there," remembers François. Clutching at any straws of hope, Jim Foley never lost faith in a deal or rescue that might save the day. Either because of his previous visits to Afghanistan or because of information that arrived in the prison, Javier Espinosa told me, Foley seems to have found out or intuited that an agreement between the United States and the Taliban for the exchange of prisoners was in the offing. He couldn't have known about the deal to free the American soldier Bowe Bergdahl for five Taliban commanders, because that happened shortly after Javier left—but he was sure that something, possibly the discreet release of prisoners from somewhere like Guantánamo Bay, would soon be afoot to get him out. "They are going to liberate some Taliban fighters," Foley said to the Spanish journalist. "The people who supported 9/11. What is the difference?" But the difference was that American soldiers, at least to their government, were worth more than American freelance journalists.

John Cantlie had always been deeply pessimistic about

their chances; now, like many of the others, he feared he'd been left for dead. Sick at what he took to be the hypocrisy of it all—he evidenced the relations between the British government and the IRA in the 1990s—David Haines even sent a desperate message for help with a hostage who he knew was going to get out. "Please, tell our governments to help us!" he implored Espinosa. "How many times have they made deals with criminals in the past? Or aren't we worth anything?"

The Iraqi sheikh, in his initial speech to the hostages assembled at the villa in Raqqa, had it wrong; Jim Foley wasn't an American soldier. If he had been, he might have had more tradable value, and might still be alive. But to Islamic State, even if a Westerner couldn't be sold or exchanged, he was still going to be worth something. "We're afraid that if they free everyone else, in the end they'll use us as scraps for their political propaganda," Peter Kassig confided to Espinosa. It was worse than that: they were going to be the main event.

CHAPTER SEVEN

Message to America

"Europeans have been released and we are still being held."

"Our governments have betrayed us."

"We have been abandoned."

By the time the hostages arrived in Raqqa, the shooting of propaganda films had become almost commonplace. The Spanish journalists were forced to appear in them, as were the French. Most of the time the words they mouthed were about the treatment of Muslim prisoners in the West, tirades against the handling of al-Qaeda suspects in offshore American military prisons like Guántanamo Bay in Cuba and Abu Ghraib in Iraq. The videos were never released publicly, but security people working the cases managed to track down a few. Some were likely intended for private consumption among jihadis; it's possible that one or two were sent to the email addresses the kidnappers had collected for their families.

But Islamic State was honing its new media production

methods all the time: by the spring of 2014, shortly after the departure of both the Spanish and the French, they were ready to make something worthy of general release. In this first film, six men, three Americans and three Brits, sitting together are asked to address the camera in turn. Jim Foley, John Cantlie, David Haines, Steven Sotloff, Peter Kassig and Alan Henning lambast the American and British governments for their failure to engage with the Islamic State to get them out. The hostages weren't being threatened with death, exactly, but neither was the video a proof of life communiqué intended only for their families or their governments. They were almost the only hostages left, and they were all wearing orange jumpsuits; every one of them knew what that meant.

No one I've spoken to has ever seen this video. The families only heard about it from the last few hostages to make it out. "There were scripts, there was all kinds of lighting," one family representative told me. "You don't care about lighting or camera angles if it's something that's just going to a family member. This was a Hollywood production. It was much more professional; and clearly conceived as a public release." It was also another sign that Islamic State was touting its British and American prisoners as a group, but it was no longer clear what they were looking for in return for their release. "When I heard about it I got scared as shit," said the same family friend. "I knew that I was just a tiny little bit of bacteria in a much scarier scene. I had no pull, or influence at that level. It was the first time I started to despair. What I was seeing was not a money thing but political theater."

By the time the video was made, the hostages had once again been moved on. Some time after the Spanish had departed, but before the French left, they'd been driven to a new prison twenty-five kilometers east of Raqqa city, near a town called al-Akershi. They'd been moved around regularly in Raqqa, but this was where most of them would stay the longest—Didier François told me he'd spent "most of the time" in Raqqa Province in al-Akershi, which meant the hostages must have arrived there in March. Their new surroundings were on a mountain, near a disused oil refinery. The prison had sprung up in a training facility known as the Osama bin Laden camp, whose intake, as well as seasoned fighters, included teenage boys whom Islamic State had recruited through *da'wah* work in the area. The whole place was heavily fortified and a military zone; by the spring of 2014 its existence was an open secret. Along with the central holding prison in the government building in Raqqa, where Peter Kassig and two of the Spanish had been held the previous winter, and the dam facility near Mansoura where they were held on their return to the province, the Osama bin Laden camp was known locally as one of the three most important Islamic State prisons in the whole of Raqqa Province. It had been listed in an Amnesty International survey the previous December. One Syrian former detainee told researchers he'd heard Islamic and military chanting during his incarceration there, as well as what sounded like a firing range.

Islamic State's approach to political theater had been years in the making. Foley and Cantlie, as the first hostages to be picked up, saw it before anyone else. The kidnappers' labored attempts to imitate the worst methods of their enemies had started with waterboarding and allusions to Abu Ghraib in the early phase of their captivity. Later it would account for the constant references to Guantánamo and those ubiquitous orange jumpsuits. "They designed the project a long time ago," Foley told Javier. "From the very beginning, the Iraqi sheikh told us, they were thinking of locking up Westerners in a high-security prison with cameras and many guards. He said we were going to spend a long time here, because we were the first prisoners they'd captured." The project had been derailed or abandoned when the hostages passed into the hands of Abu Athir in Aleppo.

Now, since the return of the Iraqi sheikh and the Beatles, they had free rein. Their obsession with Afghanistan and Iraq explained why the American hostages, and particularly Jim Foley, were given a harder time than anyone else. The visceral loathing of the Beatles' ringleader George for Jim Foley, according to some of the freed hostages, amounted to psychopathic hatred. On at least one occasion, however, the Beatles' enthusiasm for violence was too much even for Islamic State. After the attacks that followed the release of Marc Marginedas, during which Foley was held by the throat so firmly that he fainted and ended up with serious bruising to his face from the fall, one of the Beatles—most likely George—appears to have been chastised for his cruelty. "Some of the other guards came in and saw it and said, 'What's happened?' " François remembers. "It seemed that they went a bit too far because for some time things quietened down. The leadership came. There was a big mess."

Abu Athir's Dutch security chief Abu Obeida, who'd treated Foley and Cantlie with relative respect in Aleppo, seems to have been in Raqqa and popping in and out of the prisons; Abu Athir may well have been in the background too. It's possible that one of them was involved in censuring the Beatles. The unusual thing about the Brits, one of the security men who debriefed some of the hostages told me, was that "there was violence even when there shouldn't have been violence. When you're dealing with criminals, they are lazy people; they don't want to hurt you. With the Somali pirates, yes occasionally they will put a gun to your head, but they will only do that when it's necessary for the negotiations. The rest of the time they'll sit and chew khat, they'll smoke cigarettes, they'll play chess. Because usually when hostage-takers beat or threaten they do it as a pressure tactic—when the only means of communication you have is an email, then why would you bother giving the hostages a bad time? I conclude that these people were more or less in it for their own amusement, taking it out on these people, which made the violence more sadistic."

Some of the freed hostages disagreed. "It's always easy to find that our enemies are crazy or stupid," sighed Didier François. "But they are just our enemies. The problem is that some of them are not that stupid. They are very careful to keep us alive as long as they think they need it. Until they decide they will kill you, in the way they want to do it. So they will play on all the levers—they will be harder, be cooler, then harder, then cooler. They always played mind games. Some people were afraid just because of the psychological pressure, that they might be beaten will be enough." Sometimes, said François, Foley might even have been mistreated "to put pressure on the negotiations"—presumably, so that any freed European hostages would let their governments and families know how serious the kidnappers were.

But the main reason Foley was treated so badly, according

to several former hostages, had less to do with his nationality than his refusal to be cowed. "James was always one of
[George's] favorite victims," said Espinosa. "Perhaps because
the American photographer endured torture with an unprecedented stoicism." Jim Foley, François told me, "was one of
the people in the room who never gave up, who never totally
surrendered. Some of the guards really hated the fact that you
could fight them back and still ask questions; keep your own
thinking and refuse to give into them. It was not a question
of nationality, it was a question of strategy and your attitude
toward them. I think the reason Jim was taking some beatings
was to terrorize the other ones and show that they were in control." There was something primeval about it, he felt. "They act
like predators. If they think you're another predator they try to
break you, or you're prey."

It wasn't only the Beatles who had it in for the Western hostages. Pierre Torres was beaten just for maintaining eye contact
with one of the North African jailers; the point was to humiliate the hostages and reinforce their powerlessness, to make
them walk with their heads bowed as if they'd done something wrong. But the British were by the far the worst offend-
ers, and it didn't help when they found out that the hostages
were calling them the Beatles. They were taking out on the
hostages all the slights and humiliations they felt they'd suffered, while expressing their criticisms of Western foreign policy. Now they were in charge, and others were on the receiving
end. Either because of their experience in gangs back home,
or their brushes with the law, violence appeared to come naturally. "They are streetwise, used to violence—they have no
problem with it," says François.

Other hostages said the same thing. Esinosa remembered John shouting "I've spent my life on the streets" when he thought one of the hostages was trying to trick him; he took it as a reference to a rowdy, lawless past rather than a pitiful claim about youth homelessness. Just as Abu Obeida had inquired after mutual acquaintances in Brussels while he was flogging Jejoen Bontinck with electrical cables, now the Beatles were cruelly goading Alan Henning that he was next on the list to be executed while at the same time asking about life in his home city: "How are our Pakistani brothers from Manchester?" This was no longer anything about money or rote, regurgitated religion, but a misshapen perversion of politics forged in the mean streets of British inner cities. This idea of prison was an absurd Skinner box, complete with Big Brother-like surveillance, constant mind games and an indecipherable system of rules and punishments. The point was to control every aspect of their prisoners' lives, to force them into absolute submission.

In the rapidly evolving strategy of Islamic State, cameras were central. Sometimes the recording of video was nothing more than a totem of power and a way to archive the humiliation of their enemies. During his blindfolded beating at the hands of Abu Athir's men, Dimitri Bontinck told me, he thought he could feel the light of a camera in front of him. In between kicks the jihadis forced him to do impressions of farmyard animals; some time later, he says, he received a threatening message from jihadi contacts in Raqqa: "We still have that video of you behaving like a chicken." More often, video was a means to disseminate fear. To buttress their case that the aid worker Alan Henning might be next in line for execution, the Beatles joked that he resembled Ken Bigley, the British engineer who had been beheaded on camera by al-Qaeda in Iraq a decade earlier. Beginning in 2004 with the American Nicolas Berg, al-Qaeda made around eighty such decapitation videos, the victims including many foreigners. Ken Bigley was one of them, and he went to his death wearing an orange jumpsuit. In the same year, Abu Bakr Naji, one of al-Qaeda's favorite ideologues, released an online manifesto, *Management of Savagery*, in which he argued that jihadis could fashion an Islamic state out of chaos and mire the United States in so many conflicts that it would overstretch itself and have to withdraw. "The policy of violence," its author advised, "must also be followed such that if the demands are not met, the hostages should be liquidated in a terrifying manner, which will send fear into the hearts of the enemy and his supporters."

Ten years later, the machinery of new media had caught up with Islamic State's ambition. With professional video distributed to a global audience via YouTube and Twitter, the opportunity was open to amplify acts of barbarity to subjugate and terrify whole populations; to make everyone's nightmares come true. It made their collection of Western journalists and aid workers more valuable than they might otherwise have been. Shortly before Espinosa was forced to make his propaganda video, he recalled sitting barefoot in an orange jumpsuit while the jihadi known as John ran the blade of an old-fashioned sword, almost a meter long with a silver hilt, across his jugular—before explaining what it would be like to slaughter him slowly, like an animal, by making a modest incision in his neck. The Brit, he remembers, wanted to squeeze "maximum drama" from the act in order "that [Espinosa] appear terrified in the video."

The descent into abject brutality was felt most keenly by Foley and Cantlie, who'd been treated relatively well in Aleppo, and they reacted to it in different ways. Increasingly they were being treated differently too. If Cantlie's evidence about the doctor Shajul Islam had led to their kidnapping, it didn't matter now—it was Foley who took the brunt of their captors' fury. Cantlie was still in good physical shape when the others left; he was working out and not being relentlessly picked on and brutalized like Foley. When I asked Didier François about what might have been going through his mind he replied defensively, batting for his friend: "What do you know about what he thinks? It has been two years, and you think there is no way out—and everybody has betrayed you or let you down."

Cantlie was well aware, according to one freed hostage, that his partner and family were making Herculean efforts on his behalf. But more so than Foley or François, he appears to have understood that no one was going to come and get him out— that he had only himself to rely on. Whereas François used diplomacy to deal with the British guards and Foley fell back on persuasion and pugnacity, Cantlie's approach was to marshal his resources, keep a low profile and try to play the long game. There were no more escape attempts. Some of the Beatles even warmed to him. "He was another Brit," said a same security man who'd debriefed some of the freed hostages. "They liked his sense of humor."

One time, according to Espinosa, the Beatles made Foley

and Cantlie compose a song, a play on the Eagles' "Hotel California." On pain of beating, all the hostages were forced to sing it in a tasteless pantomime: *"Welcome to lovely Hotel Osama. Such a lovely place, such a lovely place. Plenty of room at lovely Hotel Osama, Any time of year, you can find it here. Welcome to the lovely Hotel Osama, Such a lovely place, such a lovely place. And if you try, and if you try, you will die Mr. Bigley-style."* But the real significance of the Ken Bigley reference seems to have been lost on the Beatles. Before he was killed, Bigley made several propaganda videos for his kidnappers, which had the effect of extending his lifespan by several weeks. To hostage-rescue specialists, his was a lesson in how to negotiate jihadi captivity. "Everybody [else] in Ken Bigley's case was killed instantly," one security man told me. "One American was killed twenty-four hours after he was taken, the other was killed after forty-eight hours, but Kenneth Bigley was kept alive for weeks. He was buying himself time—he even got to the point where he escaped, but then he was picked up." Keep talking and make yourself useful—it was as good a strategy as any, and John Cantlie might have taken it to heart.

Some time in May, not long after the group video of the British and Americans was made and while they were still in the Osama bin Laden camp, the treatment of those left behind got significantly worse. The reason was that they were caught passing notes to Kayla Mueller and the other women who were being held in a different room, possibly via a toilet which was shared by all the prisoners. "They were caught communicating," said one freed hostage. Jim Foley was very likely involved, and may well have been the instigator. The Beatles didn't need much excuse to beat their prisoners; now they had one.

*   *   *

At roughly the same time, the families were working to solve communication problems of their own. Only gradually had the Foleys and the others realized that their loved ones were all being held by the same people, that the emails they'd received had likely been written by the same man. Little by little they acquired one another's contact details and learned how to bounce ideas off each other, to share tips and slivers of information for the evaluation of everyone else. When the hostages began to come out in March and April, the urgency of their task became much more pressing. Among the Americans the idea took hold that they needed more formal coordination as a group, the better to raise the profile of the hostages and to put pressure on their government to do something. Islamic State was clearly bringing its British and American hostages together for maximum leverage; now the families were going to do the same.

Raising the profile of the hostages wasn't going to be easy. With the exception of Jim Foley, whose parents had gone public with the news of his disappearance early on, hardly anyone knew that the others were missing. The rest of the British and American families, threatened by the kidnappers and often leaned on by governments and security people too, had urged the international media to respect a voluntary "blackout" on news of their kidnappings. To some of the families it all looked too convenient, allowing governments to wriggle off the hook. "It gave the FBI a huge break," reflected John Foley.

While the British families signed up to the media blackout of their own accord, it's unlikely that they were given impartial advice on their full range of options. Hans Dyer, whose brother

Edwin was kidnapped and eventually killed by al-Qaeda in the Sahara in 2009, told me that the Foreign Office told him "not to talk to anyone—no option, no reasoning. I was kept in the dark; I wasn't pushy enough. I trusted them and I didn't interfere...I was even told that the issue might cause embarrassment to the government in the impeding election." His experience was not uncommon. Like many others Diane and John Foley were caught between an avalanche of flaky leads, that in their case could be sifted by private security people, and U.S. government agencies, which told them almost nothing at all. Diane would eventually become friendly with some of the other hostages' loved ones, and she counts her relationship with the Cantlie family as a "blessing," but she couldn't help feeling that governments wanted to keep information to themselves and everyone else apart. "They didn't want us coming together," she says. "On some occasions," the representative of another family told me, "governments were telling us—don't talk to the others."

By May, the American families had had enough. Over several days five families of those who'd been kidnapped in Syria—the four Islamic State hostages plus Nancy Curtis, whose son Theo Padnos was still held by al-Qaeda, met for a series of meetings in Washington. To get to know each other better, two of the mothers even shared a hotel room. Their first stop was the Atlantic Media Company, whose owner David G. Bradley acted as their host; he was already paying for many of the families' and their representatives travel expenses, and helping with advice and research assistance. From there they went on a tour of the different U.S. government departments to offer some suggestions and get some answers as a group. Only the immediate families were allowed into the meetings. One mother remembers the State Department as "really depressing. A windowless room, fake flowers, grim. Twelve family members at the end of this oval and twelve government members at the other end. We had to wait in silence until a big guy came in who said 'the situation in Syria is very complex.'" But the message was very clear, and she paraphrased it as follows. "The U.S. will not pay ransoms, it will not negotiate. This is the best way to protect American citizens in general."

The Washington meetings came soon after the release of the French hostages, and the Foleys were keen that the email address Didier François had brought with him should be shared with everyone, that it be acted upon in some way which might appease the kidnappers. But it had taken time to gather the families in one room, and getting governments to work together was going to be much harder work. John Foley recalls "sitting in a meeting with the FBI, the State Department people and the other non-communicating bodies there in the room. And I personally asked them, 'Have you talked to François?' 'Well we've talked to him, but he won't talk to us.' Number two I asked, 'Have you talked to the Brits?' They said, 'They do things differently than we do, so we can't work with them.'" For Diane Foley, "it was the last chance, when François got out in April. It was just the fact that us Western allies don't work together. We just don't."

But the elephant in the room was what would happen if they did. Even if the U.S. government were put directly in touch with the kidnappers by François or the French government, what would be the next step? At their meeting in the State Department the families had been told that it was a "hard and fast rule" of U.S. government policy not to pay ransoms or negotiate with terrorist groups, but the message they received at the FBI was subtly different: "Yes, it's true that the U.S. doesn't pay ransoms. But if you are negotiating with the terrorists we will sit with you in the room and we will help you with the negotiation. And we know how to bargain, we know about ransoms. We will hold your hand through this whole ordeal." It was something to think about. One of the freed Europeans had told the Foleys that the kidnappers were going to work through all the other hostages, whose countries and organizations were easier to deal with, and come back to the British and Americans when they'd finished. The Foleys needed to be ready.

By this time, John Foley had taken over the job of emailing the kidnappers. Given Arabic culture, they had been advised, a plea from Jim Foley's father might be more effective. They were still firing off emails to the address they'd been given, pointing out that they were not rich people but that they would pay what they could. There was never any reply, but it was important to keep trying. And when they worked out that the Europeans had been released for multi-million-euro ransoms—it took a while, because hardly anyone was telling them anything—they set about trying to find ransom funds on their own. "As everyone started coming out," says Diane, "we thought, wow, we gotta raise money." But it wasn't going to be as simple as that. For the Foleys it was conceivable that any K&R insurance policy made available by *GlobalPost* might cover some kind of ransom. But, starting around the time of the Washington meetings, they say, a counter-terrorism expert from the National Security Council repeatedly threatened to take them to court if they paid. They took pro bono legal advice, which said that any prosecution was extremely unlikely, but the mixed messages and confusion slowed them down nonetheless.

Even if the FBI was prepared to turn a blind eye to the payment of ransoms, it was at least hypothetically possible that any U.S.-based business or magnate lending the money could have their business shut down for financing terrorism. One workaround was to find a foreign intermediary or a friendly Arab regime to pay instead. Via the businessman David G. Bradley, efforts were made to reach out to well-heeled, Islamist-friendly Qatar—"We have to figure out who is funding these people," one family representative remembers Bradley saying—but in the case of Islamic State at least, there was no progress. "I think the Qataris didn't feel they had the kind of influence with Islamic State that they had with Jabhat al-Nusra," said Phil Balboni.

While the families were tapping up potential intermediaries and thinking about ways to pay a ransom, the FBI was quietly putting in place plans to get the hostages out by force. One reason the FBI was playing relatively nice, according to the Foleys, was because they needed the information the families were bringing into the investigation. They also needed access to the freed European hostages, some of whom would have preferred to speak to the families direct. Around the same time as the Washington meetings, some freed hostages did sit down with agents of the FBI and other intelligence agencies in various European cities and hand over information which might identify the kidnappers and, more pressingly, where they'd been held. They quickly settled on al-Akershi; the oil refinery and outbuildings were visible on Google Earth. The

FBI agents appear to have left Europe with detailed sketches of the prison and information on its roster of guards, but if a rescue mission was in the offing, they needed more than that. The hostages had been there since March, and the kidnappers were learning fast. Some time before they'd been released, the two Spanish journalists Javier Espinosa and Ricardo Vilanova were separated from the others, presumably for security reasons. When they were taken away from the other hostages in Mansoura, the kidnappers had prepared an elaborate charade to make it look like they were moving everyone on to a new prison. They'd worked a similar trick earlier, when their fellow Spaniard Marc Marginedas had left. "Get your things," one of the guards had shouted. "We're going to Iraq."

Meeting the FBI wasn't the only way the freed hostages were trying to help out. The cheap, pungently distinctively aftershave worn by the Beatles' ringleader George had made an impression on many of them, and one had the idea that it might yield clues as to his identity. On his release he took it upon himself to hunt through European pharmacies and perfumeries in an effort to find it.

The dazzling turnaround in the fortunes of militant Islamism blindsided Western governments and terror analysts. A year after its birth, as American counter-terrorism experts were threatening to prosecute the Foleys if they paid it a ransom, a distinctive entity called the Islamic State of Iraq and Sham didn't even feature on the U.S. terror list. The United States, along with almost everyone else, had lumped it in with al-Qaeda in Iraq. If the FBI was keen to talk to its freed hostages, that was possibly because Islamic State had moved so fast under its radar that they knew more about the organization than the FBI. "We survived for ten and a half months in the belly of the whale," recalls Didier François. "It gave us an insight into many things; we arrived at the first split in the movement, and we saw Baghdadi develop his strategy. We saw it first hand. We had the chance to discuss it with some of the cadres of the organization a little bit." The strategy, as François saw it, was to put aside Pakistan and Afghanistan and take back leadership of the radical Sunni movement for the Syrians, the Palestinians, the Jordanians and the Iraqis—to create a new kind of al-Qaeda in the heart of the Middle East.

In February 2014 ISIS was formally expelled from al-Qaeda for its ambitions, but that hardly mattered. The organization had already spectacularly renewed the franchise of militant Islamic extremism around the world. On new media Tunisia and Indonesia to Gaza and the Yemen, the wooden pronouncements of Ayman al-Zawahiri were being passed over for demonstrations of support for Islamic State and sightings of its distinctive white-circle-on-black flag. Underneath Islamic State's rapidly evolving new media strategy was a battle for control of the global jihadi movement—a battle it was clearly winning. Its distinctive pitch was that its new state could be a home and a place of greater safety for disaffected Muslims around the world. What it needed now were skilled professionals; the inaugural issue of the Islamic State's glossy magazine *Dābiq* made a "special call" to "military, administrative, and service expertise, and medical doctors and engineers of all different specializations and fields." The sophistication of its output on Twitter and YouTube was surely one reason why thousands of young Europeans flocked to ISIS. Another was is its transnational ambitions, married to its brio in building heaven on Middle Eastern earth. When I asked one young analyst, Aymenn al-Tamimi, to explain the lure of this Islamic state to young Europeans he simply shrugged. "A state gives you something to do, doesn't it?"

The next phase in Islamic State's development was about to unfold. At the beginning of June its fighters rolled back from Syria through the Sunni heartlands of Iraq to take the country's second biggest city, Mosul. As if to prove their point that they recognized no such imperialist carve-ups as nation-states, along the way they used bulldozers to erase the traditional boundaries between Syria and Iraq.

One afternoon in June, from my hotel room at the Turkish border, I Skyped one of Islamic State's foreign recruits, a thirty-year-old Brit who'd traveled to Syria a year earlier and who was now living in Raqqa under the *kunya* Abu Sumayyah al-Britaani. The ease with which ISIS's shock troops had routed the Iraqi army in the previous two weeks had burnished its mythology, and Abu Sumayyah was full of it. It was the only reason he was talking to me; the Islamic State's military successes were the perfect opportunity for a little *da'wah* among media unbelievers. He'd lost his British passport, he confided, but it no longer mattered—he looked forward to the coming era of passport-free travel as the Islamic state spread through Syria, Iraq and beyond. In any case, he said, he'd spent time in a British prison "for the propagation of my religion," and had no wish to go back. It had been a formative experience. "I was radicalized in prison. I learned about the Koran, about what was happening to the Muslims around the world, like in Myanmar." Talking to him was more like humoring a street rapper than interviewing a seasoned terrorist. "Listen, *akhi*," he would say; *akhi* is the Arabic word for brother and the comradely address preferred by jihadis in Syria. When the internet connection dimmed he quipped, "Bro, you sound like something from *The Matrix*." Among his new friends were jihadi veterans from Afghanistan as well as Tunisians, Brazilians, Swedish, Chinese, Mexicans, Algerians, all kinds of Europeans and many Americans. He made it sound like a Benetton ad, but with everyone wearing black. "It's like a dream: one day we eat Eritrean, the next we eat Pakistani. We are breaking borders, we are breaking racism."

They were also breaking Iraq. As the Islamists rampaged through the north of the country, the international media focused on grainy social media footage of what looked like mass executions of hundreds of their Shia militia prisoners, but Abu Sumayyah felt that the killings had been taken out of context. A full two thousand Iraqi soldiers had been given the opportunity to repent, he noted; even the Shia apostates were given a chance. "This is the way of Islam. Everyone gets a chance to repent. But if they don't, it's death. It's the same in every country in the world; it's treason against the state."[6]

He was, however, wrong about the options afforded to Shia prisoners. Shortly after we spoke, Islamic State released a

---

6. A month after we spoke, the *Daily Mail* would out Abu Sumayyah as Kabir Ahmed, a father of three who had left Derby for Syria. He had criminal convictions for stirring up hatred against homosexuals and for shouting abuse at a passing Gay Pride parade. Six months later, in November 2014, he would, according to jihadi media, blow himself up—the first Islamic State suicide bomber to come from Britain.

slick thirty-minute feature showing exactly what had become of them. In its finale, a chilling foretaste of the execution videos, a chain of young Iraqi men could be seen screaming and pleading for their lives as they were led toward a blood-soaked jetty where, in quick succession, they were forced onto their knees by masked gunmen, shot in the back of the head, and launched like dead fish into the river. The aim, just as with the Western hostages, was to subjugate and sow panic. There was no offer of repentance.

On June 19, 2014 Daniel Rye Ottosen and Toni Neukirch were deposited at the Turkish border. The twenty-five-year-old Dane had struck up a close friendship with Jim Foley in captivity; both were photographers, open-minded and curious about the world, and in the prisons they clicked. Ottosen was probably the only hostage to have had as bad a time in prison as Foley, having been tortured from the very beginning. He was in such good physical shape that the guards couldn't believe he was a real journalist, and assumed he must be CIA. The treatment was so bad that he squeezed himself out of a small window and attempted an escape. He'd made it further than Foley and Cantlie, zigzagging barefoot through cornfields while bullets whistled past, but he'd been caught. Afterward, just as had happened with Foley and Cantlie, his treatment had gone from terrible to worse; his jailers had left him hanging from the ceiling for days, suspended by handcuffs that cut deep into his wrists.

Ottosen's freedom had cost just over two million euros. Since the Danish government, like the Americans and British, baulked at giving money to terror groups, his parents were forced to beg, plead or borrow the money from everyone they'd ever met. "My case was kind of extraordinary," he told me, "because there was no government behind me. So my family had to collect all the money themselves. They needed all the network of connections—basically everything that they could get their hands on who could supply them with money." His background as a champion gymnast probably came in more useful than his new profession as a journalist, as his parents asked gymnastics groups to help. Everyone chipped in—"from the smallest to the biggest," said Ottosen proudly.

The negotiation for Ottosen's release had been under way for some time, and he and Neukirch were very lucky to make it out when they did. Islamic State's conquest of Northern Iraq had changed everything. From now on, Western powers would no longer be able to ignore its territorial expansion, and the families of the remaining hostages watched events with mounting dread. The Foleys were still working out how to raise money, and how to pay it without leaving anyone at risk of prosecution; in time Diane Foley would travel to Copenhagen to seek Ottosen's advice. The going rate for a hostage appeared to be between three and five million dollars, but the Foley camp had to assume there would be a premium on the American and British prisoners.

Before they could pay anything, however, they urgently needed the kidnappers to get back in touch. There hadn't been any reply from the encrypted email account the Foleys had been given in November. François's new email address had been lost somewhere between the French and the U.S. governments, and in any case might only have been an attempt to wind everyone up. In the absence of any direct message from

Islamic State, some of the families had long felt obliged to look into intermediaries of their own. Some were reputable and trustworthy. In the border town of Kilis, a local representative of the powerful Turkish Islamic charity IHH Humanitarian Relief Foundation told me they'd been asked to intercede on behalf of two of the Spanish hostages—to pass on a letter—but nothing seemed to have come of it. The representatives of other hostages tried IHH too. With an excellent presence on the ground in Northern Syria, it was well placed to help.

Others were not. As word got around about the Western hostages, a host of shady rebel entrepreneurs popped up along the Syrian Turkish border offering to free them, one way or another, from the clutches of Islamic State. All were worse than useless; one was Ammar Boka'i, the same rebel militia leader who'd held the Italian, Belgian, and Ukrainian journalists. Earlier that year I'd phoned to ask him what he could tell me about his role in their kidnappings. He was in Hama Province in Northern Syria, he said, and in the thick of vicious fighting against Islamic State. When we talked about the kidnapping of Domenico Quirico and Pierre Piccinin da Prata he claimed to be just another middleman; he'd been tasked to negotiate with the kidnappers and had taken only one hundred thousand dollars for himself.

As for Anhar Kochneva, he swore there hadn't been any ransom; she was simply a spy who ran away. "We were using her as a playing card to put more pressure on Russia. If I capture her again, I will send her for revolutionary trial." Boka'i was well aware a dozen or more Westerners, including Americans, were being held by Islamic State in Raqqa, and he was ready to raise an army of three thousand men to go and get them out. The only sticking point, he said, was a lack of money and weaponry; the Americans were full of promises, but hadn't given him anything. We'd made vague plans to meet, and a month later I was with several Syrian rebels in Antakya when I asked one of them to find out if Boka'i was free for an interview. Two minutes later a text came back from someone in his office: "A journalist. Great. Is he rich? Shall we kidnap him?" It was a joke, but everyone else laughed louder than me.

The market for middlemen with the Islamic State was soon crowded, too. Late one night, ten days after Daniel Rye Ottosen reappeared, I met one of them in the border town of Reyhanli. Dr. Rahhal, a bulky, professorial-looking rebel, had promised to bring proof of life for Jim Foley, but it was clear that he didn't have it. Instead he arrived with a shifty-looking wingman he claimed was a sheikh, and an ingenious solution. He presented me with two short video clips: one featured a cowed-looking Ukrainian couple and the other a man who he claimed was an Iranian spy. Both were clearly being held hostage by rebel groups or al-Qaeda, but no one was interested in buying them back—how about if he hand over one in return for some money from the Foley family, as a down payment for Jim? "Mr. Foley's family is very rich, we know this," said Dr. Rahhal. "And we know all about what he did in Libya," added his friend. As we drank our tea in silence Dr. Rahhal handed over another proof of life to confirm his bona fides, this time for an American whose name he said was Peter. The picture was of a gaunt man with heavy stubble and a faint grin, holding up a piece of paper on which he'd scribbled in block capitals: "HI MOM! MISS YOU! SEE YA SOON, INSHALLAH. TODAY IS FRIDAY, MAY 16."

It took me a while to work out who it was. Peter Curtis, whose real name was Theo Padnos, was the American free-lance journalist who'd been kidnapped almost two years previously and who'd been held for a time in the same Aleppo compound as Jim Foley and the other Western hostages. ("Oh my, doesn't he looks skinny," said his mother Nancy when I sent her the photo.) The difference was that he'd been taken by Jabhat al-Nusra; when it and Islamic State fell out he'd been dragged along on a long-winded tour of much of Syria.

Padnos was one of the very few journalists for whom a media blackout might actually have been appropriate. In 2011 he'd published a controversial book called *Undercover Muslim* about his experiences trying to understand extremist Salafi Islam in Yemen. The title alone was inflammatory—which is why, on his next visit to the region, his passport showed his mother's surname and another of his first names instead. Even as Peter Curtis he was seriously tortured in captivity. Given the paranoia of his captors about CIA spies and baseless allegations about his motives in the Arab press, there is little chance he could have made it out alive if they'd discovered his true identity. The ransom for Peter, according to Dr. Rahhal, was twenty million dollars, but his family had thus far been able to offer only fifty thousand, with the result that his case had been sent to the back of the queue. The American, he added, might soon be handed over to ISIS, a common tactic among rebel groups to put pressure on negotiations; no one who cared about anyone would have wanted them to end up with Islamic State. "Fifty thousand is small change for the kidnappers," huffed Dr. Rahhal. "His family is very poor, but what can we do?"

The Foleys were relatively lucky. While they had private investigators to whizz through spurious intermediaries like Dr. Rahhal—he was mortified, he told me, that they'd already given his proposal short shrift—some of the other families were working almost entirely on their own. The British among them, including the family of John Cantlie, had access to a facility called Hostage UK whose role was to support them and feed them information on what was going on and get their loved ones out. Freelance efforts to engage Islamic State, however, contravened the British government's bar on dealing with terrorists and were rebuffed. Other than the ear of friendly FBI agents, the American families had even less.

Without a working communications channel, and with little or no help from their governments, some families made easy prey. Later the *New York Times* would unearth a "sheikh" along the Turkish–Syrian border who claimed to be able to broker the release of Peter Kassig if the family advanced him one hundred thousand dollars. At around the same time the *Guardian* would break the story of an attempt by the New York lawyer and former radical Stanley Cohen to get Kassig out by leveraging his old contacts among al-Qaeda clerics in Kuwait and Jordan. The sheikh claimed to have a letter of authorization from Islamic State, and a photo of himself with Ottosen the day he was freed. Two young friends of Kassig had gone along to meet him near the Syrian border, and been forced to size him up on their own.

Nothing came of any of it. The sheikh might well have had a photo, and might even have been employed to drive Ottosen to the border, but he was most certainly not the intermediary used by Islamic State—because, when it came to its Western hostages, they weren't using local intermediaries. Neither was there any real evidence Stanley Cohen's al-Qaeda contacts had any pull with Islamic State, not least because by then the two organizations were bitter rivals. The sheikh wanted a hundred thousand dollars and Stanley Cohen was shortly to go prison for taxation offenses. For the families, it was one of the worst things: being pulled this way and that by a succession of middlemen motivated by money or kudos and who, even if their motives were entirely benign, usually offered nothing more than false hope and distraction.

One of the more useful pieces of advice thrown up by the K&R industry was the need to keep a real line of communication with the kidnappers open, and avoid extraneous noise. "In every kidnapping case," reflected Didier François, "you spend more time closing doors than keeping them open, than negotiating. It's very easy to open a channel—what's difficult is to keep that channel open without other interferences, not to fuck up with your negotiations. To brush away all the people who think they know, who pretend they know." It was another sign of the growing professionalism of Islamic State, and its impressive facility with new media. Unlike almost every other kidnapping outfit in Syria it used email addresses to reach out to families directly and cut out the middlemen—to keep negotiations on its own terms, and all the proceeds for itself.

Shortly after midnight on July 3 locals heard the lumbering roar of helicopters swooping in low and moving fast through the Raqqa countryside. Such was the noise that the remaining

Western hostages might have heard it too. At various points in their captivity some of the hostages had heard what they assumed were explosions from Syrian regime air strikes; perhaps those left behind assumed this was more of the same.

This time, however, they were American Black Hawks. They were backed by fighter jets and surveillance drones circling in the night sky, and this whole armada was headed in the direction of al-Akershi. Their first task, on crossing the border into Syria, would have been to knock out any anti-aircraft batteries between them and the camp. Then, with a wall of covering fire in place, some of the Black Hawks touched down and several dozen commandos—a combination of U.S. Army Delta Force and Navy SEAL commandos—dropped out and hit the ground running. They began, according to local activists, by cutting off the road linking al-Akershi to Raqqa. After that they fought their way into the Osama bin Laden camp, exchanging fire with Islamic State militants as they went. With night-vision goggles and heavy-duty military equipment the Americans must have looked conspicuously out of place, pushing through door after door and building after building, clearing them in turn.

The hostages were not there. It was always going to be a tall order to get them out by force, and the U.S. Army might well have been wary of another Somalia—with images of American soldiers being dragged through the streets—or a new version of the failed 1980 Delta Force mission to free American hostages in Iran. But the timing and intelligence were also questionable. The Black Hawks appeared more than three months after foreign hostages had arrived in al-Akershi, and two and a half months after the first of those hostages had been released back into the world. They also came a fortnight after Daniel Rye Ottosen had been freed at the Turkish border. Along with Toni Neukirch he had been the last hostage over whom the kidnappers were in active negotiation; it was the perfect time to move everyone else on. Given their previous security precautions and the regularity with which they'd been secreted around prisons in Raqqa, it was inconceivable that the kidnappers wouldn't have taken *any* steps to cover their tracks.

"They must have had something, it was a fucking big risk," one security man told me. But it's very likely that they didn't— that the raid was precipitated by the news of the severity of the hostages' situation, and their worsening treatment. Time was running out, but then time had been running out for months. After news of the raid leaked, officials in the U.S. administration admitted to the *New York Times* that there had been no specific intelligence that Foley, Cantlie or the others were still being held where the raid took place. A Special Forces officer told a reporter from the *New Yorker* that the intelligence was "a little bit stale" before adding that "you couldn't *not* take a swing." In retrospect the whole thing looked less like a rescue attempt than a clunking gesture, a message to Islamic State that it was no longer untouchable.

If it was, it didn't have much effect: Islamic State's campaign on Iraq showed no signs of abating. On August 7, as it threatened Kurdish areas of the country, President Obama announced targeted air strikes on its positions in the country to protect American interests and throw a lifeline to the Yazidis, a local ethnic Kurdish population that was under immediate threat. Four days earlier, and in just a few hours, Islamic State had swooped in to take control of their whole area. As

word spread about the brutality of the Yazidis' new masters—
to the Islamists they were devil-worshippers who would have
to be killed, converted or taken as slaves—tens of thousands
of them fled their homes to the protection of nearby Mount
Sinjar.

Together with the failed raid to get them out, the air strikes
that followed sealed the fate of Jim Foley and the others. After
them the Islamists were likely hurting, and the hostages were
the only tool at their disposal with which to hurt America
back. More than the United States, however, they also seemed
to know that a war against their old enemy was coming, which
is why—after that initial ransom offer, which may well have
been genuine—they'd kept the American and British hostages
back. And in the age of new media, they had a better understanding of their propaganda value. If they couldn't be sold for
money, they could always be fed into the Islamic State's gory
propaganda machine. A week after the rescue mission, another
jihadi who'd spent time in London and who arrived in Syria at
the same time as some of the Beatles posted a tantalizing message to his Twitter account: "Message to America," it read. "The
Islamic state is making a new movie. Thank u for the actors."

The video of Jim Foley's killing would be titled "A Message
to America." The decision to kill him and the others might,
however, have been arrived at months before, one family
representative told me, at around the time the kidnappers
recorded the group video of their British and American prisoners. "I think there was a decision to execute them all way
back when. It was all an effort to get UK and the U.S. mired in
another conflict; I think they wanted to embarrass these countries, and make a big media thing out of it after letting all the

other countries' citizens go. They were dragging it out. They just decided on a different communication strategy, one by one rather than as a group—executed a little differently."

As to why they started with Foley, a security man thought he knew the answer. "They took the most valuable hostage they had in terms of media attention, and they decided to kill him. They wanted to leave this message out there for the entire world to see." Didier François thought they'd chosen Foley for a number of reasons. "I don't know who took the decision," he told me. "It is difficult to say. The Iraqi sheikh in charge didn't like him, so the guards didn't like him. It was a combination of things. His personal standing during detention brought more attention on him, and they saw that maybe he would have the biggest impact on U.S. policy and public opinion because he was well known. And because there was no negotiation, it was their best option." The plan might have been in the making as early as when Foley and Cantlie arrived back in the custody of the Iraqi sheikh and his British accomplices. It likely hadn't escaped their attention that Foley was one of the first two prisoners to arrive in their own private Guántanamo. "They are not boy scouts," added François.

If the kidnappers knew their remaining hostages were not going to be allowed to leave, some of their hostages strongly suspected it too. John Cantlie had long realized that this wasn't going to end well. As their captors' rage against America in general and Foley in particular intensified, he must also have understood that his good friend and companion was in more immediate danger than himself. Daniel Rye Ottosen was another pessimist. "They don't fucking need the money," he told me after his release. "From the beginning they were interested in hitting America. The demand for money was not a demand, not serious. This is a war against America. The more they can do to stick the needle into America the better. If that means letting Europeans go because they want to cooperate... but [they think] America is evil, evil, evil."

Some of those freed earlier in the year had been permitted to take with them letters for the families of those left behind. As their numbers grew thinner and the guards more suspicious, that became less of an option—and the Foleys, to their chagrin, never received any letter from Jim. Together Foley and Ottosen decided that, if the latter was ever released, he shouldn't carry a letter in case it was confiscated. Instead they'd prepare one orally and he'd memorize it. The letter developed over time, as did its contents; then, shortly before Ottosen left, they rehearsed it. In its own way, it was another attempt to beat the control freakery of their guards. But both men also knew that Ottosen might be the last to make it out, and they wanted Foley to have a message of his own. On June 20, twenty-four hours after his release and as soon as Ottosen arrived back in Copenhagen, he phoned Diane Foley and recited it to her:

Dear family and friends,

I remember going to the mall with Dad, a very long bike ride with Mom. I remember so many great family times that take me away from this prison. Dreams of family and friends take me away and happiness fills my heart.

I know you are thinking of me and praying for me. And I am so thankful. I feel you all especially when I pray. I pray for you to stay strong and to believe. I really feel I can touch you even in this darkness when I pray.

Eighteen of us have been held together in one cell, which has helped me. We have had each other to have endless long conversations about movies, trivia, sports. We have played games made up of scraps found in our cell…we have found ways to play checkers, chess, and Risk…and have had tournaments of competition, spending some days preparing strategies for the next day's game or lecture. The games and teaching each other have helped the time pass. They have been a huge help. We repeat stories and laugh to break the tension.

I have had weak and strong days. We are so grateful when anyone is freed; but of course, yearn for our own freedom. We try to encourage each other and share strength. We are being fed better now, and daily. We have tea, occasional coffee. I have regained most of my weight lost last year.

I think a lot about my brothers and sister. I remember playing Werewolf in the dark with Michael and so many other adventures. I think of chasing Mattie and T around the kitchen counter. It makes me happy to think of them. If there is any money left in my bank account, I want it to go to Michael and Matthew. I am so proud of you, Michael and thankful to you for happy childhood memories and to you and Kristie for happy adult ones.

And big John, how I enjoyed visiting you and Cress in Germany. Thank you for welcoming me. I think a lot about RoRo and try to imagine what Jack is like. I hope he has RoRo's personality!

And Mark…so proud of you too, bro. I think of you on the west coast and hope you are doing some snowboarding and camping, I especially remember us going to the Comedy Club in Boston together and our big hug after. The special moments keep me hopeful.

Katie, so very proud of you. You are the strongest and best of us all!! I think of you working so hard, helping people as a nurse. I am so glad we texted just before I was captured. I pray I can come to your wedding…. Now I am sounding like Grammy!!

Grammy, please take your medicine, take walks and keep dancing. I plan to take you out to Margarita's when I get home. Stay strong because I am going to need your help to reclaim my life.

Jim

CHAPTER EIGHT

The Living and the Dead

Shortly before ten o'clock on a damp New England morning, hundreds of Jim Foley's family and friends filed into Our Lady of the Holy Rosary Catholic Church in Rochester. The memorial service took place exactly two months after Foley had been led out to be killed. If he'd been alive, it would have been his forty-first birthday. His body was still somewhere in the sands of Raqqa, but a photo had been mounted on the altar. From the pulpit Michael Foley, who'd done much to help in the search for Jim, delivered a rousing tribute to his brother. "I'll never make complete sense of why Jim died," he began, "but that is not for me to understand. But he did not die in vain." Katie, the last member of the family he communicated with in that internet café nearly two years earlier, read from the Book of Wisdom. Father Marc Montminy, who'd known Jim Foley since he was a child, presided over the service, and spoke warmly of Jim's ability to give voice to civilians trapped by war and violence.

After mass there was a private graveside service for family and close friends, and then people moved to the banqueting hall next door for lunch. Everyone was invited. In the early evening the family arranged a private dinner at a nearby school, and it went on until late. It was another celebration of his life, both joyful as well as sad, and everyone spoke informally about their memories of Jim—photos, including some of his work, were projected onto a big screen. Daniel Rye Ottosen, who brought Foley's last letter home, made the journey from Denmark and said something too. He remembered how he taught Jim massage and how, even though he wasn't very good at it, they'd keep at it just to pass the time. The pair would also have arm-wrestling contests, at which Foley was the stronger.

Another of those who spoke in Jim's memory was his editor, Phil Balboni. A gracious man, slow to apportion blame and always ready to listen to anyone who might help, he'd been a constant presence in the Foleys' lives during Jim's captivity. Two days after the funeral mass I met him at *GlobalPost*'s airy waterside offices in Boston. The place was spartan and businesslike, nothing like the traditional newsroom—its kind of intrepid reporting no longer seems to reap huge rewards. After his kidnapping in Libya, Foley had worked there as a desk editor, and Balboni pointed out which had been his chair. It was great to have Foley around, he said, but it was also clear that he was bored and anxious to get back into the field; at one point Balboni had joked about taking away his passport. Most of the journalists and aid workers who subsequently dashed across the border into Northern Syria were freelancers, frequently pushing the envelope of what was possible to make sure they got paid at the other end. Even though he did most of his work for *GlobalPost*, Foley was the same. Whatever their faults these courageous men and women went to where even spies feared to tread to shine their torch on a terrible conflict.

When the hunting season came along, with no access to armed guards or panic buttons, they made easy prey. For the journalists it must have been galling to think that they'd become pawns in a much larger game, to think that they were considered more valuable as hostages and candidates for ransom than for any of the reporting they would bring back. It was their bad luck, because some of them were the most resourceful people it was ever possible to meet. Like many of the others, Jim Foley had been kidnapped before, and knew how to turn almost any situation to his advantage. Austin Tice's close friend Christy Wilcox, herself a freelance journalist on Syria and one of the last people to speak to him before he went missing, told me that in the bizarre propaganda video which surfaced after his kidnapping he might well have been playing along with his captors in an attempt to win their trust. "My instinct is that maybe both sides here were playacting, that he was befriending them and doing what was necessary to protect himself." The same hope came up again and again at the end of my interviews with journalist friends and families: "If anyone can make it back, they can."

But many of them didn't. Could things have been any different? "I would say James and John went from something very terribly awful," reflects Didier François, "to something amazing, strange but sort of OK, then back to something more

difficult but not as bad as it was before, then after I left I think
it became a bit worse. And in the end they were in deep shit."
It's an elementary rule of K&R that the best chance to get the
hostage back is to move in fast with the right information; it's
how John Cantlie came to be freed the first time. The private
security team working for *GlobalPost* were on the ground admi-
rably early, but were quickly distracted by the idea that Foley
and Cantlie had been taken by the Syrian regime.

Whoever the "very credible confidential sources" who convinced them that Foley and Cantlie had been taken by the Syrian regime were, they were willfully, dangerously blind to the
complexity of the conflict then brewing in Northern Syria. It
was the best reason to have freelance, independent journalists spending time there—to find out, beyond the histrionics of
TV news and the smoke and mirrors of social media, what was
really going on. Hindsight, of course, is easy. The Brits involved
in taking Foley and Cantlie were vicious people, and the bal-
ance of power between different rebel groups had shifted
since John was first held hostage. They were now organized in
a semi-professional kidnapping gang; even with all the right
information it might not have been possible to get them back.
But it would have helped if the investigators were looking in
the right place.

As soon as hostages arrived in Aleppo, any attempt to get
them out by force was going to be more difficult. Islamic State
was simply too well dug in. Certainly by the time they were
taken away to Raqqa the only way to get them back was by
negotiation—which the British and American governments
were never going to do. Whoever was responsible for his email
channel falling by the wayside François, like some of the other

European hostages, thinks that the British and Americans were simply abandoned to their deaths. Some security people tend to agree. "I totally get that funding terrorism is not a good thing," one K&R professional who's worked Syria cases told me. "But when you're in a position where there is a life at stake, it's like first aid. You know that some of the first aid is not necessarily good for you—like shoving a pencil through the throat to make you breathe, for example—but it's life-saving. So where I come from we pay that money, we keep that negotiation running, we buy ourselves time, we create an opportunity to maybe get this guy out through another means."

Not even the Foleys suggest that one hundred million euros should have been delivered to Islamic State to save the lives of three Americans and three Brits. Their argument is for a more nuanced, smarter approach. Diane Foley bemoans that the authorities "didn't bother to use the intelligence properly when they got it. So they could make a successful raid. Or they could engage the enemy through negotiation to see if there was some way. We just don't think that happened, and it saddens us hugely. I thought the British and Americans were rather shrewd. I mean Scotland Yard and the FBI, right? We've really got to study this group, and we've got to be shrewd."

On September 24, 2014, a month after Jim Foley was killed, the American State Department placed Amr al-Absi, or Abu Athir, under whose authority Foley and Cantlie and most of the other hostages seem to have been gathered in Aleppo, on a list of ten Specially Designated Global Terrorists. "As a principal leader of ISIL in Syria," read the communiqué, "he has been in charge of kidnappings." At the time of writing, both he and the Iraqi sheikh appear to be at large and very likely still in positions of authority in Islamic State. The State Department noted that al-Absi had been selected as provincial leader "for Homs, Syria, in the Aleppo region"; Homs, as Foley, Cantlie or any other freelance journalist in the area would have been able to tell them, is not *in* the Aleppo region.

Whatever confidence Jim Foley had that serious measures were afoot to get him out appears to have been misplaced. Until they began to be publicly slaughtered, the lives of the American and British hostages just weren't worth very much to their home governments. "What we found is that people don't want to help," a representative of one of the other families told me. "They have their own independent ends which they pursue. The lives of the hostages fell between these cracks." It's issues like this that the Foleys plan to address in the James W. Foley Legacy Fund they have set up to honor his memory. Diane Foley takes comfort from the camaraderie and the friend-ships Jim forged in prison, and his efforts to bring everyone together. Didier François remembers Foley as "a fantastic fel-low, and fellow hostage. I liked him very much. He was one of the key pillars." The freed European hostages told John Foley that "Jim was the best at moving his soul, his spirit, outside the box. And I think that that's what he was able to do. To persist, and pursue." Foley told Daniel Rye Ottosen that in prayer he felt closest to his family. He also said he could do another year, if that's what it would take to get him out.

Two others in attendance at Jim Foley's birthday memorial were Theo Padnos and his mother Nancy Curtis. After I left the offices of *GlobalPost* I strolled through downtown Boston and sat in the waiting room of the dental clinic where Nancy was having some work done. Out came a laconic, silver-haired lady in trainers, loudly paying her bill and arranging her next appointment. "When is Theo coming in?" asked the receptionist.

Theo Padnos and Jim Foley had a great deal in common. They crossed over from Turkey into Syria at roughly the same place and were kidnapped only a month apart, in the autumn of 2012. Just like Foley, Padnos had been forced into an orange jumpsuit, and to make propaganda videos castigating the American government; for a time they'd even been held in the same compound in Aleppo. Before they turned to journalism both had been writers and had taught in American prisons; it might have helped both of them endure their captivity for so long. They even grew up in roughly the same place. "They were outdoorsy, from northern New England, where it's really beautiful like the American West," says Nancy. "And they were both public-spirited." And yet one was alive and the other one dead. Five days after the video of Jim Foley appeared, on August 24, 2014, Theo Padnos was released. The timing can hardly have been a coincidence. It's highly likely that Foley's public death concentrated minds and spurred Theo's handover to the United Nations peacekeeping force in the region. "The Foleys are so generous," Nancy told me. "It must have been difficult to see Theo, but they embraced him as if he were their own."

For Nancy Curtis, the terrifying experience of having a loved one kidnapped in Syria had begun exactly two years earlier. A bookish museum administrator, her first encounter with American law enforcement officials hadn't gone well. "I called up an FBI boss and said, 'My son went into Syria a week ago, and he's disappeared—I think something terrible has happened and I don't know what to do.' And the guy said,"—here Nancy raised her voice to a boom—" 'Lady what do you want me to do? I didn't ask him to go to Syria.' " The next time she called, she was assigned to a female FBI agent who was more sympathetic. When ransom demands in the region of twenty million dollars began to arrive, it was clear to Nancy, just as it had been to John and Diane Foley, that the kidnappers wanted to talk to the American government and not her.

In her case, however, that's exactly what happened. "It began with my FBI agent and the chief negotiator flying to Turkey to meet with the Nusra representative." The representative claimed to be an intermediary of some kind, but it was clear to everyone that he was involved. Two FBI women, according to Curtis, met him "in some neutral location. They wanted to find out if the ransom demand was authentic." As soon as they established that it was, they stood back and let Nancy and an Arabic-speaking friend of hers get on with the job of negotiating with the kidnappers. But at each stage in those communications, which took place via the internet, Nancy's assigned FBI agent was in the same room to give them advice. Nancy's pitch was to plead poverty. She confirmed that her initial offer had been fifty thousand dollars; via her Arabic-speaking friend she claimed that she was old, that she'd sold all her furniture and that she was now reduced to selling her clothes. "We were working with the FBI," she told me. "They said, 'Bid low, it's like buying a rug.' "

None of it worked, but it kept the kidnappers talking and a line of communication open. It was while when the negotiations were going nowhere that several photos and videos were made of Padnos, including the one I'd sent to his mother. Later that week I visited the family home and Theo, a dreamy, naturally inquisitive writer-adventurer like someone from an earlier era, told me the story of his kidnapping in person. He also told me how the photo I'd received had come about. One day a man called Abu Marouf al-Homsi had wandered past his cell and smiled in his direction. "I'm out here in the sticks too, and you and me are buddies," he told Padnos. "I'm going to get you out." Soon afterward he ushered Padnos into a separate room, asked him a series of proof of life questions that could only have come from his mother and then took his picture—the same one I'd seen. Just like Dr. Rahhal and many others, Abu Marouf was setting himself up as a market-maker and freelance intermediary. But like all the others his proposal was a non-starter—the money on the table wasn't nearly enough. "The issue," Theo told me, "was that everyone was dealing with chump change, so everyone would come back to the big sheikh, Abu Maria, and say, 'Sheikh—I was able to get x or y or z.' And he'd say, 'Get out of here; I need the big cash.' "

In the end, Padnos was only released because the American businessman David G. Bradley, acting on Nancy's behalf, made a personal appeal to Qatar, the same tiny but very rich country that had brokered the release of Bowe Bergdahl from the Taliban, which has been generously funding Islamist rebels in Syria, and which might even have helped France funnel ransom money to Islamic State. After Padnos's release the State Department claimed it followed "a direct request from the Curtis family itself to the Qatari government for its assistance," but it was clear that someone in the U.S. government must have quietly given the nod, and in a hurry. "Of course I'll never know," says Nancy Curtis, "they will never say—but there were people in the United States who helped." The Qatari official she spoke to denied that any money had changed hands: "We're more nimble than the United States," they'd said. But it stretched credulity that al-Qaeda kidnappers who'd demanded twenty million dollars and brushed off more modest offers would have parted with their only American hostage for nothing.

Like Jim Foley, Theo Padnos was treated badly from the beginning; the worst of it came after his cellmate Matthew Schrier escaped, when he was roundly and gruesomely tortured for weeks. As usual they wanted Padnos to confess he was CIA; with all his fluency in languages they assumed he had to be. (They weren't the only ones. After his time in Yemen Padnos was dogged by lazy rumors that he's some kind of intelligence agent. "He couldn't have been CIA, his Arabic is too good," a U.S. official commented to Nancy after his release.) Thanks to all the beatings and malnutrition, he suffered multiple concussions as well as serious problems with his teeth; it was why Nancy was trying to line up dental appointments for him. He still has difficulty sleeping. In the end the kidnappers decided that they liked Padnos, but that was only because the Qataris were showing interest and they could sense a payday in the offing.

In retrospect Theo blames himself for his naïveté in going in the first place, but we Syria journalists were all a little naïve. "This whole thing, money for life, it's so obscene," reflected Nancy, but she'd played a very good game as a negotiator. The cruel reality is that hostages have become a key card in modern warfare, and that once someone is taken they become a weapon in someone else's hands. And in the end, and if they really want someone back, everyone deals. Everything else, including drawing lines in the sand about never talking to terrorists, is just another negotiating strategy, and not a very good one. No one else does it. In his jihadi prison cell Padnos met scores of Syrian soldiers waiting to be swapped or to have ransom paid. "There was a spectrum of ranks, but there were seventeen officers of the Syrian army in my prison cell. And a senator." What happened to them? "They let them go— or they kill them. I think they would have let me go; it would have taken longer but they would have let me go eventually." His mum interrupted to scold him: "I think they'd kill you tomorrow."

After Jim Foley the videos kept coming, every two weeks and with a trailer for the next hostage to be executed at their end. Steven Sotloff, David Haines, Alan Henning—all of them apparently killed by the same British kidnapper known as Jihadi John. Six weeks passed, and then the body of Peter Kassig showed up at the end of another grisly performance in November. It became almost routine. In January 2015 two

Japanese men, one a freelance journalist and the other a troubled adventurer, were killed in quick succession after a cursory financial demand from the Japanese government. At the beginning of February Islamic State took its choreographed horror to new heights with a film of a Jordanian pilot being burned alive in a cage. But the gruesome series showing the decapitated bodies of British and American hostages seemed, at least for a time, to have stopped.

There was hardly anyone left. "The narrative is played out," one family representative told me, bitter disappointment in his voice. For many it was a crushing end to what seemed like an eternity of waiting; after all their efforts to track down proof that their loved ones were alive, all they got was proof of their deaths. Islamic State had known the value of their hostages better than their own governments. If they couldn't be traded for money they could just as easily become fodder for a new kind of propaganda spectacle. They also understand that, in the age of ubiquitous new media, media blackouts on kidnappings could be turned to their advantage. When anyone could break a blackout with a camera and a YouTube account, it handed a loaded new-media gun, and the initiative, to the kidnappers.

John Cantlie seems to have understood this too. A month after Foley's execution, videos and articles began to appear in which he talked about his life in captivity, poked fun at the enemies of Islamic State, and bemoaned the British government's lack of interest in getting him out. These were scripted messages in support of his kidnappers, but their delivery closely mimicked formats already familiar in Britain. An essay he wrote for *Dābiq* was titled "Hard Talk," and was clearly borrowed from the flagship BBC program of the same name. In one of a series of faux news broadcasts Cantlie was taken to the Kurdish enclave of Kobani in Northern Syria, which was then under attack by Islamic State militants, to make a film about the progress of the fighting. Just like the lurid YouTube murders, the intended audience wasn't Arabic- but English-speaking, and particularly young European men. "These are street kids, we must insist that Cantlie is cool," one of the freed hostages insisted. It was the only way he could imagine that his former cellmate might emerge with his life.

What John Cantlie was doing was enormously courageous, and clearly the right thing to do. With his comrade Jim Foley and the others gone, feeding his captors' appetite for slick new-media propaganda was the only way to persuade them to keep him alive. "Once we were finally put into general population with dozens of European prisoners," he wrote in one of his articles for *Dābiq*, "we had to watch them all go home to their loved ones while we, the British and Americans, were left behind. That was a bitter pill to swallow, but nothing compared to what came next. Now I've had to watch as James, Steven Sotloff, David Haines and Alan Henning walked out of the door, one every two weeks since August 18, never to return, knowing they were going to be killed and going to their deaths... What does that do to a man?"

Didier François chose his words carefully. "Everyone chooses their own survival strategy. I have not been with John for more than six months, so it would be very arrogant of me to try to judge, or explain why he says this—if he is forced to do this, or if he's trying to save his life. He doesn't believe that his government is going to negotiate for him. He is trying to survive; he is walking a very thin line." Some of Cantlie's friends and loved ones said the same thing; that he would do whatever it took to stay alive. "John is resourceful," one told me, long before anyone even knew who'd kidnapped him. "He could play the game if he was with Islamists and might get out." Jeroen Oerlemans, the Dutch photographer who was held hostage with Cantlie the first time, had total confidence in his friend's judgment. "Big John is a media-savvy guy—he knows how to sell a message. I think he is performing, giving them what they want, but doing it in his own way—and that's what makes him valuable for them. You could mistake him for being sincere about this, and there is some truth about what he is saying [about being abandoned by his government]. He is not a stubborn guy. He's completely focused on survival. I think that he thought this up."

At around the same time as Jim Foley's birthday memorial came an intriguing postscript to Cantlie and Oerlemans's first kidnapping. When their usual fixer Mustafa hadn't been able to make it to the border that day in July 2012, he'd sent along his young cousin Durgham instead. Durgham had escaped and raised the alarm, but after it was all over locals began to suspect that he might have been involved. It's not clear whether he really was complicit—the Islamists were abusing him as much as they were the two Europeans—but the experience, coupled with a subsequent falling-out with his family, seems to have affected him greatly. He joined Jabhat al-Nusra, and from there migrated to Islamic State. According to Mustafa, Durgham became an important figure in the organization: "I tried to talk to him many times, but he threatened me." If Durgham found out that John was back in his area six months later, he might well have tipped off his radical Islamist friends. Not long after John Cantlie was fronting his film about Islamic State's successes in Kobani or shortly before, Durgham was, according to Mustafa, killed in the fighting there. His death came at the hands of an American-led air strike; part of the same campaign on Islamic State's Syrian positions that the death of Jim Foley had helped bring about.

Another casualty of those air strikes was the aid worker Kayla Mueller. As a woman Kayla had always been put in a different category by the kidnappers. In July 2014, long after the kidnappers had stopped asking for money for the British and American men, her family had received a ransom demand for five million euros. But there was no easy way to pay it—and as soon as the others began to be slaughtered it was taken off the table. Shortly before I went to Boston I phoned her boyfriend Omar al-Khani and he put it succinctly. "If they don't want to pay, there is no other way to bring them back. [But] where can we can find a rich man who can pay six million dollars, and who isn't American?"

In February her family received proof that she'd been killed in Raqqa. Islamic State claimed that she died in one of the air raids, but it's just as likely that they engineered her death to punish America. With a ransom no longer an option and presumably no propaganda value to be had from decapitating a young female aid worker on camera (the kidnappers could easily have slaughtered her like the others if they'd wanted) it may have been the only use she had left—to embarrass the American authorities.

The cycle of kidnapping never ends. The air raids that precipitated Jim Foley's death were, at least in part, to save an imperiled group of Yazidi Kurds who live in the shadow of Mount Sinjar on the Syrian edge of Iraq. They seemed to work, but in their immediate aftermath the men from Islamic State moved into local villages and kidnapped between three and five thousand people. Many were women and children; at the time of writing, most are still missing.

Three months after the memorial service for Jim Foley, in the winter of 2015, I traveled back to Iraq and Northern Syria to interview Yazidi refugees and visit those who were still huddled on Mount Sinjar. Almost everyone I met had had someone kidnapped; some were missing whole branches of their extended family. A few had been able to keep in touch with their loved ones by mobile phone, at least at the beginning; others were entirely in the dark about whether they were dead or alive. Some had been stolen away, like the Western hostages, to the Islamic State headquarters in Raqqa. But others, more disconcertingly for the Yazidis, were being held only a short drive away by men they'd once considered neighbors.

Under Islamic State's martial theology, the kidnapped Yazidi women had become spoils of war, to be used as slaves for housework and worse. By then, so had Kayla Mueller. On another trip I traveled to two different refugee settlements in Northern Iraq to meet the two teenage Yazidi girls who'd shared a prison with Mueller in the two months immediately after Jim Foley's execution. One girl had had to tell Mueller the news of his grisly execution on video: "He was my friend," she said, crying. Both remembered Mueller praying and taking instruction in the Koran from an important visitor, who was also having her brought to his bed and raping her under the flimsy sanction of an impromptu marriage. They knew him as Abu Khaled, but when I showed them pictures, both identified him as Islamic State's leader Abu Bakr Baghdadi.

The Islamic State franchise is still gathering momentum, and will likely be with us for some years to come. The genie is out of the bottle: even if it's toppled in Syria and Iraq, it can pop up elsewhere. Its supporters are good at reciting from their holy book, but their success had nothing to do with their interpretation of religion. It came about through chaos and statelessness, when legitimate complaints were allowed to congeal into religious grievance and then harden into demands for the stabilizing hand of puritanical law.

Unlike al-Qaeda, who only wanted to blow things up, Islamic State also wants to build something. At the beginning, when they saw this collection of tiny emirates mushrooming around their country, some Syrians dubbed them "The States"—a kind of United States of Jihad. Its appeal was never a mysterious Syrian or Iraqi thing but more universal; to some disaffected young people and others with nowhere else to go, an Islamist utopia might seem worth a try. To do anything about it is going to require some serious thinking, and for everyone to work more purposefully together.

The same goes for political kidnapping. Much like the rise of Islamic State, it's a symptom of what happens when things fall apart. Long before they took to kidnapping foreigners, Islamic State was involved in the wholesale kidnapping of Syrians for modest amounts of money. It still is. One young Yazidi I met in Iraq had been contacted two days earlier by someone claiming to represent Islamic State and demanding twenty thousand dollars for his sister. He had no way of knowing if it was a genuine offer. At a refugee camp so waterlogged that moats had formed around some of the tents, another young man called Salah Hassan buttonholed me about how sixteen members of his family were still missing; he patiently reeled off who they were. "Our thinking has stopped. We don't know what to do. We are fluctuating between hope and despair," he said.

After the Western hostages political kidnapping is finally a story, and likely to become even more of one in the years ahead, especially for Americans and Europeans who venture to dangerous parts of the world. So is the question of what to do about it. Less secrecy and a lot more sharing of information would be a good start. "Kidnapping," the family representative of an executed Islamic State hostage told me, "is this odd thing which draws in so many different sectors of society, brings so many things and kinds of people together, and it reveals how little in agreement we are with each other. And how unwilling people are to adjust their own ends for the good." It also throws into sharp relief the differential value of human life. At one point in time Islamic State was holding twenty-four Western hostages. In only one of those twenty-four cases, two Syrians died trying to find information that might have got the hostage out; one was killed by regime shelling in the course of his work, while the other was shot at an Islamic State checkpoint. It's very likely other Syrians were killed, too, putting themselves in harm's way to bring back people whose lives were clearly worth more than their own.

The brutal calculus of kidnapping leaves little room for heroes, and no moral argument for almost anything that passes for a response. But the unavoidable fact is that some hostages are more valuable than others, because the chilling effect of their mistreatment and murder has the power to send a message. At an unofficial border crossing in Northern Iraq I took a flat metal boat to cross into Syria with some refugees who were headed back home. A family jumped in behind me and, as we wobbled free of the harbor, I crouched down to take some pictures of their children. Through the lens I focused on a boy of about six who was smiling back at the camera. Still grinning he pointed toward Syria with his index finger and then drew it back sharply to make a slicing movement across his throat. It was either a joke or a warning, but it can only have referred to what happens to journalists in the Islamic State.

A Note on Sources

Syria is a black hole. Given the enormous difficulties in getting safely in and out of the country, anyone can say what they like about what goes on there. And they do. Since it's extremely difficult to investigate anything amid the chaos there, standards of evidence and credibility tend to be more relaxed. A good deal of the reporting from second-hand sources on Syria since 2011, even in serious newspapers, has been simply wrong, or the truth bent so far out of proportion as to be unrecognizable. All the more reason to have skeptical, independent journalists like Jim Foley spending long periods of time there to find out what's really going on.

The same goes for reporting about the rise of the Islamic State. Much of our information about Syria and the rise of IS has been filched from nakedly partisan activist sources or from the rumor mill of new media. Then there are the "analysts" or unnamed "intelligence sources" or "diplomatic sources," most of whom have never been to Syria and have borrowed their information from the previous two. To make matters worse, in Syria new media has become a weapon to be pointed at one's enemy like any other. Too often our approach to foreign conflicts is to pay people to be our friends, and in return those people—often desperate to get their message across, or simply desperate for money—tell us what they, and what we, want to hear. The sound of axes being ground—by governments, political activists, intelligence agencies, security interests, NGOs and other interested parties—can be deafening. Poor reporting of Syria based on partisan or compromised sources has done untold harm to Syria and our understanding of it. By further aggravating hatred between the warring parties and fooling early rebels about the military prowess of their own side, I think, it's gotten many people killed.

Reporting the Islamic State's kidnapping campaign runs up against more specific problems. Media "blackouts" about kidnappings always claim to be in the interest of victims but often just protect governments, commercial or institutional interests—and greatly hinder our understanding of events on the ground. When some European hostages of the Islamic State were released at least some were strongly advised not to speak to the media by the governments or agencies which had paid for the release. Most were debriefed by intelligence agencies or other interested parties; those who paid for their release effectively paid for that information, and kept it to themselves. There is a lesson here. Despite what the internet evangelists say in the brave new world of digitized data, information does not want to be free at all. Real information, unlike the fountain of online chatter which penny-pinching news organizations use to fill up their papers, is more expensive a commodity than ever—and getting more so.

What is a reporter to do? None of what follows claims to be definitive; the only person alive who can tell us about the kidnapping of Jim Foley is his friend John Cantlie. If he ever gets out, as I hope he does, he will have the story of a lifetime. In the meantime I've done my best to get as close as possible to events by interviewing everyone around all these kidnapping cases. In many reporting trips inside Syria since 2011 I've traveled with Syrian civilians, under the protection of a wide variety of different rebel groups, and under civilian or journalist visas stamped by the Syrian regime. I've done my best, as I think journalists should, to be skeptical of everyone and everything I've been told. Since early 2013, when I began researching kidnapping in Syria, I've interviewed about a hundred foreigners and Syrians who've been kidnapped or arrested in Syria by Islamist or other rebel groups or the Syrian regime; probably more so than any other Western journalist. In total this book draws on hundreds of interviews, either in person, or over the phone or Skype. Every single one of those interviews has been recorded and transcribed; in many cases, I've conducted follow-up interviews to better establish the facts. In the interests of transparency I've named as many Syrian names as possible; even if their surnames are rebel noms de guerre, everyone knows who they are.

My research for this book included some European hostages who were released by the Islamic State in the spring of 2014. A few spoke to me on the basis that I shouldn't use their names at all. Others were ambiguous as to whether they wanted to be named; yet others were clear they wanted our conversation to remain off-the-record while the Islamic State was still executing their friends at regular intervals, for fear that being named in a report might do more harm than good. Again in the interests of transparency, and since too often our reporting of Syria is hampered by anonymous sourcing and conflicting information, I've taken the decision to name as many names as possible for this book.

The reporting is still far from perfect. Some of these European hostages were with Jim Foley and John Cantlie for only a few months, and weren't in a position to know everything about what had happened before or afterward. Many were not in a position to know about the bigger picture—about who was organizing all this, and why. Some of them disagreed about some of the facts, which made my job more difficult. A good many freed hostages just didn't want to talk to me, and not only because they'd been sworn to silence. Some simply decided not to do so until their remaining hostages, which at the time of writing John Cantlie and one female aid worker, were safely back home. I could understand their reasons. All I can say is that I've done my best to join the dots and scratch away at the story, drawing on as much testimony as I could glean and leaving out as little as possible. While on a tour of rebel-held Aleppo City in Spring 2013, I later discovered, I unknowingly passed the joint Islamic State and Jabhat al-Nusra (al-Qaeda) prison where some of the Western hostages were held. Two years later, in the summer of 2015, I persuaded Syrian pro-regime paramilitaries to take me to a former Islamic State prison outside Aleppo City, a wood or furniture factory in an outlying industrial district, where I'm convinced most of the Western hostages were held in the Autumn of 2013.

To fill in the gaps I also sat down for face-to-face interviews with security men and women, both American and European, some of whom who were directly involved in debriefing some of the freed European hostages. Those interviewees all requested anonymity, for understandable professional reasons, which I've respected. In the book I've been careful only to use such "security sources" in relationship to the facts of their debriefing of European hostages; too often security and intelligence sources have their own axes to grind, and from which journalists should retain a healthy skepticism. In any case, intelligence and security people weren't the only ones to debrief or otherwise talk to the freed hostages. Some family or friends of the remaining hostages did so too, as official on-the-ground representatives of their missing loved ones. I've interviewed some of these family representatives, and gotten to know some of them, and have also respected their request for anonymity.

Some Notes by Chapter

Six weeks after Jim Foley's death, his parents John and Diane generously agreed to give me two detailed interviews in London for the purposes of my research for *Vanity Fair*, which I use in the prologue for this book. In the same prologue I identify the date of Jim Foley's killing as August 18, 2014. The execution video certainly appeared on YouTube on August 19, 2014 but appears, according to an article John Cantlie wrote in captivity for the fourth issue of the Islamic State's magazine *Dābiq*, and presumably written under duress, to have been filmed twenty-four hours earlier on August 18—which would mean that it took just twenty-four hours to produce and be uploaded to new media accounts around the world. "Now I've had to watch as James, Steven Sotloff, David Haines and

Alan Henning walked out of the door, one every two weeks since August 18th, never to return, knowing they were going to be killed and going to their deaths," Cantlie wrote. In the fifth chapter I quote the "Iraqi Sheikh" as telling John Cantlie shortly after his kidnapping in that "to go through this, you will need a heart of stone." This comes from the same article, as does the quote from Cantlie which begins, "Once we were finally put into general population with dozens of European prisoners" in chapter eight. *The Economist* article referred to in the prologue was published under the title "Back to Iraq" in the September 13, 2014 issue of that magazine.

In chapter one the name and identifying features of "Yasser," who also appears in subsequent chapters, have been altered for his own safety. In chapter one, the article I co-wrote with Marie Colvin for the *Sunday Times* appeared in the *Sunday Times* on February 5, 2012 and was titled "Bombs fell like rain. You could only pray; As the Syrian opposition steps up its attacks on the regime, a stand-off in the city of Homs claims more than 200 lives," by Marie Colvin, Peter Kellier and Annasofie Flamand. (Since I was traveling two weeks later on a civilian visa to Damascus, I wrote under the pseudonym Peter Kellier). Also in the first chapter, the paragraph about the early days of the Syrian revolt draws on material I collected for *The New Republic*, "The Stalled Revolution," which was the cover story of its April 19, 2012 issue. The story of my brief arrest by the Syrian army is expanded upon in a dispatch I wrote for *The Atlantic Monthly*, which appeared under the title "Hard Laughs" in its June 2012 edition.

Some of the material about kidnappings in the first and second chapters draws on my initial investigation for *Vanity Fair* magazine which appeared in its May 2014 edition under the title "Evaporated." The material on Austin Tice comes from a wide variety of rebel sources who met him on his epic progress through Syria, or who helped secured his path inside the country. In chapter two, the account of the day of Jim Foley and John Cantlie's kidnapping in November 2012 is drawn largely from face-to-face interviews with their fixer and their taxi driver on that day, in Antakya and Beirut respectively. For their own safety they are identified only by their first names, Mustafa and Abdulkader respectively. Various K&R professionals spoke to me about the nature of Syria work for this and subsequent chapters; all requested anonymity. The British journalist taken by forces loyal to the Syrian regime shortly before the kidnapping of Foley and Cantlie also requested anonymity, both for him and his employer. The paragraph about my return to rebel-held Aleppo City in the spring of 2013 draws on material collected for *The Nation*, which was the cover story under the title "The Battle for Aleppo" in its June 24, 2013 edition.

In the opening paragraphs of the third chapter, some of the material from my discussions with Abu Nabil appeared in a magazine feature I wrote for *GQ*'s November 2014 issue in the UK, under the title "Into Hell." Here again, the K&R investigators I spoke to for this chapter requested anonymity. The account of that eagle-eyed Canadian woman identified in this chapter as having first discovered that Austin Tice video was verified by another volunteer working on the case. She requested anonymity, as did John Cantlie's partner. The new material on Austin Tice's kidnapping comes from rebel sources inside Darraya and other Syrian towns where Tice spent time before he went missing, all of whom I interviewed and re-interviewed by phone or Skype over many months. In chapters three and four, the material about Firas al-Absi and his brother Abu Athir is based on half a dozen face-to-face interviews with rebels and rebel activists on the Turkish–Syrian border over several years, as well as follow-up phone and Skype interviews to try and check that information.

The material on the early Islamic State prisons for foreign hostages in chapter four is based on the combined testimony of a number of freed European hostages, as well as on interviews with several people who debriefed those hostages and the testimony of the Belgian jihadi Jejoen Bontinck. Extracts from the video of Choukri Ellekhlifi on the streets of London before he left for Syria were broadcast by Channel 4 News in the UK in March 2015; the full video remains with me. Some of the material on the Sheikh Najjar prison in chapter five is based on a report on the prison which featured on Syrian pro-regime television in the Summer of 2014, combined with my visit to the same prison in the Summer of 2015. Several interviews with Omar al-Khani helped to clarify the layout and location of that prison.

In chapters five through seven, some recollections of life in the Islamic State prisons for foreign hostages in Aleppo and Raqqa borrow from Javier Espinosa's four-part account of his own detention at the hands of the Islamic State, which appeared in his own paper, the Spanish daily *El Mundo*, in March 2015. I followed that up with email correspondence with Javier, to request some clarifications. My material on the latter prisons in Raqqa comes from interviews with some freed European hostages and a variety of people who debriefed those hostages. In chapter five, the "visiting American" who'd worked alongside ARK spoke on condition of anonymity. In chapter five, the communication from the kidnappers to the family of Peter Kassig is taken from Lawrence Wright's reporting on the same subject, published as "Five Hostages" in *The New Yorker*'s July 5, 2015 issue. The young Syrian woman who Steven Sotloff met and asked to accompany him inside the country, and who turned him down because of the risks, requested anonymity too.

In the paragraphs about the role of middlemen in the Islamic State kidnappings in chapter seven, the articles referred to are "The cost of the U.S. ban on paying for hostages," *New York Times*, December 27, 2014 and "The race to save Peter Kassig," *The Guardian*, December 18, 2014. In the section about the failed raid to get the hostages out, the articles referred to are "In raid to save Foley and the other hostages, U.S. found none," *New York Times*, August 20, 2014 and "Inside the failed raid to save Foley and Sotloff," NewYorker.com, September 5, 2014. In chapter eight, the information about the death of Durgham came from his cousin Mustafa, and was independently relayed to me at around the same time by a Syrian journalist who'd been in touch with Durgham before he died fighting for the Islamic State.

Acknowledgments

The idea for this book sprang from a series of open-ended commissions from *Vanity Fair* magazine over several years, which allowed me the time and resources to investigate kidnapping in Syria. I'm indebted to the magazine and my editor there, Cullen Murphy—at a time when freelance journalists are regularly exploited or disowned in conflict zones, both he and *Vanity Fair* are a class act. I'm also grateful to Christopher Cox at *Harper's* magazine, who commissioned several features from me looking at Syria and the rise of the Islamic State. Funding to set aside time to write the book, along with a previous grant which enabled me to spend time as a fellow of the Reuters Institute at Oxford University, came from the Airey Neave Trust. Again, I'm grateful to its administrator, Sophie Butler, and all its trustees. Needless to say: the conclusions which I drew from my investigation, along with any errors, are entirely my own.

Funding and expert logistical support for two long reporting trips to rebel-held Syria and Turkey, and then to regime-held Syria, to research the rise of Islamic State came from Tom Hundley and Katherine Doyle at the Pulitzer Center on Crisis

Reporting. Another reporting trip to Northern Iraq and rebel-held Syria for the same purpose was funded by the Nation Institute's Investigative Fund, where Sarah Blustain provided editorial advice and patient logistical support. Thanks to them all. Some of the reporting in the book draws on my earlier writing about Syria's descent, commissioned by a range of magazines and newspapers. I'm grateful to former editor of *The New Republic* Richard Just, Kate Julian at *The Atlantic Monthly*, Roane Carey at *The Nation*, Melissa Denes at *The Guardian* magazine, Bronwen Maddox and Jonathan Derbyshire at *Prospect* magazine, Cordelia Jenkins at *Newsweek* and Stuart McGurk at *GQ* in the UK. Daniel Soar at the *London Review of Books* generously commissioned an investigation which fed into this book in its early stages. Ben de Pear of Channel 4 News and Ben Plesser of NBC News worked with me on European jihadis and the Islamic State, as did David Rose at the *Mail on Sunday*; my thanks to them too.

Six weeks after the death of their son Jim, his parents John and Diane Foley were generous enough to allow me two long face-to-face interviews; I can't thank them enough. Dozens of journalists, most of them freelancers, gave me interviews or contributed their advice or expertise about kidnapping, Syria, and the rise of the Islamic State group. I'm particularly grateful to the former hostages of ISIS and Jabhat al-Nusra who talked to me; and to the families, close friends, and representatives of hostages who were still being held captive at the time I spoke to them, or who didn't come home. Arno Vanden Eynde helped me translate court documents from a trial of Belgian jihadis in Antwerp; the lawyers Kris Luyckx and Gareth Peirce were generous with their time. Sotto voce gratitude to the security people and current or former intelligence officers who spoke to me on condition of anonymity. Most of all I should mention my enormous debt to the very many ordinary Syrians who helped my reporting, acted as impromptu translators, gave me interviews—or who guided me inside their country, often illegally and for little or no reward, and took phenomenal risks to keep me safe.

My editors at Little, Brown in London and at Hachette in the United States gave excellent advice on how to make the initial manuscript more readable, and then worked very hard on editing it, checking errors and generally making it look more like a lovely book. Given the topical nature of the subject, it was great to have their speed and efficiency as well as their expertise.

The late Bridie Kelly, my aunt, was an invaluable source of encouragement over many years: the book is also dedicated to her memory, and to her sister the late Mary Bradley. My sister Emma, as always, was a fantastic help; thanks also to friends Stephen Foley, Adam Curtis, Clare Collins, Mark Johnson, Dominic Rubin, Sharon Kinsella, Kitty Hauser, and Yasmin Whittaker-Khan. And to Hazel Ingrey for her presence and her patience, and for making everything worthwhile.

Index